SPEEDRUN

The Unauthorised History of
Sonic The Hedgehog

Julian Hazeldine

Speedrun: The Unauthorised History of Sonic The Hedgehog Copyright © 2014 Julian Hazeldine.

ISBN: 978-1-291-84338-5 (Hardback)
ISBN: 978-1-291-83188-7 (Paperback)
ISBN: 978-1-291-83234-1 (ebook)

British Library Cataloguing in Publication Data
A catalogue record for this book is available from the British Library.

First published in Great Britain in 2014   (2)

Front cover illustration by YF Studio

SPEEDRUN

The Unauthorised History of Sonic The Hedgehog

Julian Hazeldine

Contents

The Seventh Generation Years (1996 – 2012)

Into The Future (2013 -)

Introduction

The funny thing is, the *Sonic The Hedgehog* titles aren't actually my favourite series of video games.

While it would be an exaggeration to say that I'd kill for a new *Project Zero* survival horror title, I would probably be willing to maim for it. Looking further back in time, a significant proportion of my childhood was spent crouched in front of a PC monitor, joining my friends in a game of Chris Sawyer's simulation masterpiece *Transport Tycoon*. But sight of the Master System incarnation of Sonic was what persuaded me to take up video games as one of my hobbies, and I've followed the character avidly ever since. Even during his salad days on the Mega Drive console, Sonic's commercial success never felt quite as assured as that of many other long-running characters, and considering the fate of his parent company over the last two decades, it's a pleasant surprise that so many of the minds behind the character have been able continue chaperoning his development.

Adding to this feeling of precariousness is the knowledge that the unique balancing act of a high-speed platforming game means that even fully-fledged big-budget Sonic titles are never more than a couple of missteps away from descending into an unsatisfying quagmire. This issue goes beyond the usual problems that beset high-profile video games, rushed to market in time for the crucial Christmas launch window. You'd be hard-pressed to find a poorer piece of software than the Wii's *Sonic and the Secret Rings*, placed on sale early one summer with no apparent urgency.

Despite this, the character has that indefinable quality that makes you actively wish his lesser ventures were better than they are. A few years ago, an up and coming clothing designer released a collection inspired by the series' trademark Green Hill Zone level, explaining to baffled fashion journalists that she'd made this choice "*because Sonic The Hedgehog is the DUDE!*". Part of this appeal is due to the time of the character's creation. Sonic came into being at a point when video games' artists were finally able to design without technical constraints. Nintendo's mascot Mario wears a hat because his hair never looked right in the low-resolution graphics of 1981, and sports a moustache to cover the inability of the computer hardware to satisfactorily render his nose. At the end of the eighties, advances in technology were sufficient to end years of game designer frustration. The result was the most distinctive and well-crafted icon that the medium has yet produced.

The initial draft of this book was somewhat opinionated; the finished article is even more so. Sonic's fans have always been passionate, but recent years have added organisational skills to their qualities. The result is several comprehensive online Wiki resources, capable of furnishing exhaustive detail on any given topic. *Speedrun* cannot match such archives for depth, but instead specialises in picking out trends emerging across the character's ongoing development, as well as providing a robust critical assessment of each element in the emerging story. Those seeking a more dispassionate history of the character will be richly rewarded by picking up a copy of Les Editions Pix'n Love's *The History of Sonic The Hedgehog*, released in the English language by Udon Publications.

As an unauthorised guide, *Speedrun* is free to be more judgemental, and crucially includes the TV shows, comics, novels and various pieces of additional fiction which prove highly instructive in assessing the character's creative direction. You may notice some instances where I refrain from passing comment on a particular product, reflecting the fact that I haven't played/watched/eaten it. I've followed the character through nearly all of his escapades, but there are some gaps in my knowledge. In such instances, I skirt briefly over the topic so that you can still follow the ongoing thread.

Before we begin, one final ground rule. This book is written from the perspective of a British Sonic fan, and the terminology used is consistent with that territory. As a result Sega's 16-bit console is called the Mega Drive, and Sonic's arch-enemy is, initially, at least, named Doctor Robotnik.

Still here? Splendid. Let's go!

The Mega Drive Years

(1991 – 1995)

1. Three Men and a Hedgehog

Sonic The Hedgehog's origins begin in a surprisingly cold-blooded fashion. In late 1989, Sega's senior staff were deliberately seeking a mascot character which would allow the company to go toe-to-toe with Nintendo for domination of the home console market.

Service Games was founded in 1940, relocating to Tokyo in 1951. A merger saw the firm rebranded as Sega in 1965, and it continued to strengthen its hold on the coin-operated amusement market. The company began marketing its wares to home users in 1986, with the release of the Master System games machine. While more technically-advanced than its nearest competitor, the device was only able to capture a small percentage of the market, which was dominated by the rival Nintendo Entertainment System.

Sega had enjoyed a moderate amount of success with its Mickey Mouse platform games (in the sense of software featuring Disney character, rather than poor quality efforts). The licensing agreements involved presented a drawback, however, and there was an obvious need for the company's own character. The chimp-like Alex Kidd had spearheaded a number of titles on the 8-bit Master System console, but Sega had faced a constant struggle to differentiate its slow-moving hero from his obvious inspiration; Nintendo's Mario.

A dedicated development team was formed to work on the title, to be released on the firm's new 16-bit hardware, the Mega Drive home system. Ideas were drawn from a wide range of pitches, with a competition being held in the Japanese company to devise its new star. Sonic's evolution was a gradual process, with early designs being based around a rabbit (for speed) and an armadillo (for the ability to roll into a ball and attack enemies). This development of the character's attributes from gameplay elements is perhaps the most important factor in making the hedgehog a complete entity, overcoming the contrived and corporate-driven nature of his origins.

Many of the prototype designs from this period have since been introduced into the Sonic games as separate co-stars, most obviously the armadillo concept. The note inscribed on the first sketches of a hedgehog translates as 'Mr Needlemouse', and the character was referred to as both SegaSonic and Supersonic in the period before his final name was selected.

More than any other entertainment medium, video games are a collaborative endeavour, but credit for the character's creation has been chiefly apportioned to three gentlemen: designers Naoto Ôshima and Hirokazu Yasuhara, together with programmer Yuji Naka. These figures were the leading lights of Sega's AM8 development group, quickly dubbed Sonic Team. It may sound odd to also give credit for character creation to the title's coder, but Sonic as we know him was tailored around gameplay

Key Game

Sonic The Hedgehog

Release : 1991

Origin : Japan

Global Sales : 4.34m

elements. Little touches such as the way the protective gold rings are scattered when the character is hit by an enemy or hazard, and the high speed at which he moves, would have been impossible without Naka's technical expertise.

Naka himself regarded his greatest achievement for the game as being the implementation of the optional rotating special stages. In later interviews, he took pride in recalling how the concept had been dismissed by many of his colleagues as impossible. Most of the game presented semi-naturalistic locations, but the special stages saw Ôshima and Yasuhara adopting a surrealist tone in creating mazes which Sonic navigated in search of the six Chaos Emeralds. The determining factor for the title's gameplay was the designers' strong conviction that it should be possible to control the hedgehog using only one button and the directional pad. This focus on accessibility to new players would serve the series well over the years, removing many of the barriers to entry which had discouraged new players from persevering with the fiddly *Alex Kidd.*

In addition to the triumphs of the hedgehog's design and speed of his movements, the third key element of the success of the title was the strength of concepts behind each level. Every location felt like a real and unique place. Much of this is due to Masato Nakamura's soundtrack, vindicating the decision to hire the composer behind the Japanese band Dreams Come True to provide the game's score. Credit must also be given, however, to the level designers for having the discipline to only use certain gameplay gimmicks in one environment. Star Light's seesaws, the Spring Yard's moving blocks and the Marble Zone's volcanic geezers meant that certain actions would only be performed in particular locations.

Although the visual design of each area now looks rather clunky compared to the more streamlined visuals that would grace later titles, it still does the job of establishing an immediately identifiable setting. You'd never confuse one level for another, even at a brief glance. It's telling that the inclusion of a very obvious level select cheat, requiring only a few button presses at the title screen, didn't dampen the game's appeal.

The 'zones' were places that gamers actually wanted to visit again and again, not mere challenges to be overcome. The sheer joy of moving at speed proved a greater drive to replay than the side-mission of obtaining all the Chaos Emeralds to watch a more upbeat ending sequence. It was only Sonic's opposition which didn't appear to respect the zone barriers, with the different types of homicidal robot Badniks sometimes deployed in a variety of settings. This somehow added to the impression of them as an invading force, rather than a natural part of the environment.

The boss encounters at the end of each area made them even more memorable, with the animal-enslaving mad scientist Doctor Ivo Robotnik usually manipulating one particular aspect of the zone's architecture in a bid to crush Sonic. The only exception is his deployment of a wrecking ball affixed to the underside of his Egg-o-matic flying vehicle at the end of the Green Hill Zone, but this wasn't the designers' intention. The ball was originally a mid-zone gameplay element, with a sequence where Sonic would have to run down a hill away from it being cut due to a lack of time in which to complete the code.

Looking at the original design of Robotnik, it's striking how clean-cut the character appears. The first sketches of the moustachioed scientist that Ôshima created were musings on a possible hero for the piece, and it's only during direct looks-to-camera that the in-game sprite takes on a malevolent expression. The design is deliberately simplistic, with a vivid red shirt and yellow braces making the villain an obvious counterpoint to the cream and sky-blue Sonic.

Sound design is generally strong, helping to make the connection for players between the visual appearance of items and their function in the game. Although the 'ring' effect is not as pure a note as the audio cue used when Mario picks up a coin, it's more distinctive and memorable. The TVs that Sonic smashes to obtain power-ups are a brilliant piece of visual design, giving a uniform appearance to the items while allowing the inclusion of a simple indicator showing what each does. Although the styling of the restart lampposts wouldn't be complete until the second of the core titles, the basic concept is present, with something that changes as Sonic runs past it being perfect for a marker of progress.

One aspect of the original game that has persisted virtually unaltered through subsequent titles is the logo. If you look at almost any Sonic product released by Sega, you'll see that the hollow of the letter 'o' is italicised, carrying an echo of the character's shape when rolling at speed. This consistency of brand management is the sort of touch normally associated with the cast-iron control of the character that Sega of Japan would eventually exert. Surprisingly, it's equally to be found in the first half of the nineties, before such micro-management became prevalent. In any case, this quirk is unlikely to have been included under Japanese auspices, being absent from the character's name in that territory (literally, "Sonikku za Hejjihoggu"). Sega of America initially attempted to use a more elaborate logo, with the character's species displayed in a red swoosh below his name, but this was outlived over the years by the subtler 'o' element.

The basic battle being fought across the game, with Sonic striving to free various smaller animals imprisoned by the mad scientist, had universal resonance. The title became a smash hit for Sega, even in the inferior form of the game released in Europe during June 1991. A poor conversion to the European PAL television format drastically reduced the speed of the title, which shared a number of bugs with the US iteration released on the same day. For example, in the west Sonic would die instantly from contact with spike traps, instead of simply losing his rings. A fixed version followed for the Japanese market, which also included a number of additional effects and animations, but it was in the west that the character quickly showed signs of becoming a phenomenon. Sega moved rapidly to capitalise on the surge in Mega Drive sales that followed.

Although Sega's 8-bit Master System console had sunk without trace in the US, it remained a viable proposition in Japan and Europe. As a result, Sonic's debut adventure was adapted for release on the machine and its portable Game Gear incarnation.

The work was carried out by an entirely separate team from developer Ancient, and was released a year after the Mega Drive version. In terms of tone and art direction, *Sonic The Hedgehog* 8-bit is perhaps best described as "inspired by" the original game. It makes a number of adjustments, including replacing half the levels with new concepts and, intriguingly, using a series of maps to chart Sonic's progress towards Robotnik's hideout.

It isn't just the forced simplicity of the game that distinguishes it, but a less brash artistic style generally. That said, technical factors result in the gameplay being almost completely different. The title is a conventional platform game, with emphasis being on slow and careful movement, and some rote learning of the levels necessary to make progress. It's still a remarkable game by weaker systems' standards, and deservedly sold many copies, but it's a very different animal to its big brother.

There's still much that's unknown about the circumstances of *Sonic The Hedgehog* 8-bit's creation, a point underlined in late 2013 by the Sonic Retro hacking forum. Users managed to uncover a music track and some gameplay assets related to the Marble Zone, one of the levels exclusive to the Mega Drive title. That area's trademark lava floods would have been impossible to achieve on the 8-bit hardware, but there were clearly ambitions at some point in development for as close a conversion as possible of the original title.

For a while, it seemed that Sonic Team's first game would also be its last, with the group splintering to the extent that Yuji Naka actually left Sega. Over the years, there have been many stories of how prickly the programmer is to work with, and opinions are divided as to whether it was a lack of status or his salary which had disillusioned the coder. The noticeable success of Sonic in the west left the company's American division in no doubt of the need for a sequel to the breakout hit, and they began attempting to lure Naka to return and head up development.

While these negotiations were ongoing, Sega of Japan's high-ups decided that they wished for their unexpectedly successful character to serve as a selling point for the proposed CD-based add-on for the Mega Drive. Several members of the original Sonic development team were drafted in to create the resulting *Sonic The Hedgehog CD*, with Naoto Ôshima directing the venture. The game saw another straightforward face-off between Sonic and Robotnik, who this time was attempting to harness the time manipulation powers of the "Little Planet" moon that periodically appears in the skies of Sonic's world.

Key Game

Sonic The Hedgehog CD

Release : 1993

Origin : Japan

Global Sales : 1.5m

Although the game was released after the Mega Drive's *Sonic The Hedgehog 2*, it's much more understandable creatively if considered first. Besides, its plot clearly places it before Naka's true sequel, which left Robotnik marooned in an isolated location. The title is notable for its unique gameplay mechanics, as straightforward linear progression through each zone will result in the player seeing only a fraction of the game's maps. Instead, the challenge is to use the various Time Posts scattered around each act to visit an earlier era of the level, and destroy the machines which Robotnik has dispatched to change history.

The non-linear level structure proved to be a one-off experiment, and these days the game is better remembered for introducing two new characters that have become an indelible part of the franchise. The design of the Metal Sonic enemy that Robotnik has constructed is simply inspired, giving life to the concept of a badnik that can counter each of the hedgehog's abilities. Although destroyed at the conclusion of his Stardust Speedway dual with Sonic, no-one believed that we'd seen the last of the android, and he would go on to return to the series many times.

The other addition was Sonic's young female (hedgehog) admirer, Amy Rose. Kidnapped whilst appearing in an early level, Sonic's rescue of the character is an afterthought in the game, with Rose only briefly appearing in one of the animated cartoon sequences which bookend the action. These movies are a key selling point of the title, and for years were looked to as the definitive guide on how Sonic should move when freed from the limitations of 16-bit sprite technology.

Sonic The Hedgehog CD serves as an interesting example of the lack of creative control which exerted over the character globally in his early years, with the various regions of Sega free to present the game as they saw fit. The most noticeable example of this is in the soundtrack, which was discarded almost entirely for the US release. The Japanese version has a central theme for each stage, which appears in a remixed form according to the time period the player is located in. The US version scrapped most of these tracks in favour of completely different compositions, while retaining the 'past' music. It's fashionable to praise Naofumi Hataya's Japanese soundtrack, but both have their strengths. The western *Sonic Boom* main vocal theme for the game is a much better effort than the *Sonic Warrior* song found in the Asian version.

The second alteration Sega of America made was less obtrusive, but also less artistically-driven. The character of Amy Rose was renamed in the manual as Princess Sally, the annoying co-lead of a US Sonic cartoon series which we'll be looking at in Chapter Four. This action was somewhat undermined by Sega Of America's inability to edit the in-game sprites, resulting in a change of name only. Given the visual differences between Amy and Sally, it's far from clear why they bothered.

In many ways, the game is a parallel sequel to *Sonic The Hedgehog 2*. It took the original game, including its engine and Sonic sprite, and tried to expand the previous title's gameplay, as opposed to *Sonic The Hedgehog 2*'s "bigger and faster" philosophy. Although many fans praise *Sonic The Hedgehog CD* as the summit of the series, it's actually rather weak.

The scavenger hunt mechanic, seeking time-jumping robots, doesn't work. The player is forced to firstly locate a Past Post, then find a suitable place for a time-hopping sprint, and finally track down the two smashable gizmos located in the past version of the stage. It's a tedious and unnecessary distraction from the simple joy of movement, which renders the future location completely pointless, as there's no gameplay reason to visit it. Weak level design is the final nail in the coffin, with Quartz Quadrant and Wacky Workbench in particular being simply dull to play.

Fortunately, on the other side of the world, Yuji Naka was having rather more success in recapturing the first game's magic.

2. Sonic 2's-day

While Sega Japan was happy to allow a more experimental approach to its new mascot, Sega of America was under no such illusions. Mega Drive consoles were selling like hot cakes: the reason was obvious, and a sequel to *Sonic the Hedgehog* was urgently needed. The US subsidiary took the re-hired Yuji Naka, and placed him in charge of a rookie development team at its Sega Technical Institute. Naka was fortunate enough to persuade Hirokazu Yasuhara to join him in emigrating to America, and the designer resumed his level layout duties at the reinstituted Sonic Team.

Despite an extremely short nine-month development period, *Sonic The Hedgehog 2* evolved to be the definitive game in the series, becoming the title that everyone thought the original had been. Recognising that the virtual locations on offer had been one of the main

Key Game

Sonic The Hedgehog 2

Release : 1992

Origin : USA

Global Sales : 6.03m

draws of the first game, the sequel offered a greater number of shorter levels, with the number of 'acts' reduced to two per zone. The introduction of the standing-start Spin Dash acceleration manoeuvre was emblematic of faster-paced and more immediate action.

Another change was made in light of the public's attachment to the character. The only piece of conscious storytelling in the first game, where Robotnik unexpectedly drops Sonic from the Scrap Brain final area back into the hazards of the Labyrinth Zone, was considerably expanded upon. *Sonic The Hedgehog 2* shows how its hero moves between the final set of locations, using the newly-introduced Tornado biplane to attack Robotnik's Wing Fortress base. A further sequence at the end of that level dramatises him then hitching a ride to the orbital Death Egg, the Star

Wars-parodying ultimate weapon that Robotnik has been constructing throughout the game.

Technical limitations appear to have forced the abandonment of an earlier cut-scene, in which Robotnik would have demonstrated the Death Egg's power by a laser strike destroying the Metropolis Zone. Sonic and his new sidekick Tails would then have to fight through the ruins of the city to reach the Tornado. Sadly, the second version of Naka's Mega Drive graphics engine wasn't up to coping with the visual swap that would be needed for the resulting Genocide City Zone. The idea was dropped and the completed level designs were used to form a third act of the Metropolis, with the mid-stage apocalypse notion later remounted in *Sonic The Hedgehog 3*'s Angel Island Zone.

Speaking of Tails, the main expansion of the gameplay concepts from the original was linked to the fox properly known as Miles Prower. (It's surprising how many people don't notice the truly terrible pun in the character's name). In one-player mode, the default option has Tails dogging Sonic's footsteps, using his helicopter-tails flight ability to catch up when the hedgehog inevitably zooms away from his companion. The arrival of Sonic's mechanically-minded sidekick was a clear statement of intent, expanding a solitary experience into one that featured anytime drop-in co-operative gameplay, to use today's vocabulary.

Having a second player controlling the fox was highly advantageous, as his infinite lives meant that he could bear the brunt of Robotnik's improved array of badniks with impunity. This was just the tip of the iceberg, however, compared to inclusion of the most comprehensive split-screen versus mode the series has seen. The contest pitched Sonic and Tails against each other across a number of stages, with the eventual victor judged on a broader array of categories than a simple race result. Power-ups used and gold rings collected were also taken into account in scoring each contest.

There are several interesting artistic shifts from the previous title. Robotnik's Egg-o-matic flying vehicle has a more Heath-Robinson feel than in other appearances, being visibly cobbled together from various disparate components. In contrast to the semi-coherent journey around South Island that the first game offered, the levels here are ordered for visual and gameplay diversity. The opening idyllic Emerald Hill is followed immediately by the smog of the Chemical Plant. Originality of the level concepts is maintained by the slight twists that are placed on the core ideas that return from the first game. For example, Emerald Hill has a significantly more tropical feel that the original title's Green Hill, and the Metropolis is less industrial and more of a city than its Scrap Brain 'metal stage' predecessor.

The largest shift was toning down the surrealism of the Special Stage. The technical enhancements across the whole title meant that the game didn't have to resort to such cheap tricks to give a drastically different feel to the areas from which Sonic recovers the Chaos Emeralds. The camera was positioned behind Sonic, as he peeled down a ring-strewn half-pipe. A more tangible reward for retrieving the gems was provided this time around in the form of Super Sonic, a chaos-energy-infused version of the hero.

As would become an established convention, the indestructible yellow avatar of the hedgehog was underplayed in the game. While additional-fiction versions of the character see him both elevated to near omnipotence and reduced to a blood-thirsty psychopath, Sonic Team seemed content to treat Super Sonic as a simply more powerful version of its lead character. While his animations suggest him to be capable of flight, he's firmly anchored to the ground, and his use constantly diminishes the player's number of rings. If the tally falls to zero, Sonic reverts to his usual self.

Masato Nakamura again supplied the music for the title, later going on to re-work the ending theme as the vocal track *Sweet Sweet Sweet* on his next album. This Japanese influence on the game was an exception to the generally Americanised tone of the franchisee at this point. While the European release of *Sonic The Hedgehog* had retained Ôshima's linework for its box art, the publication of the sequel saw a painting by American artist Greg Martin adopted. The prolific Martin would come to define Sega of America's house style, but his depiction of Sonic and Tails stood in front of a large '2' is probably his most famous creation.

Unsurprisingly, there was a massive marketing push for the game's launch, with the US release date dubbed "Sonic 2's-day". Although *Sonic The Hedgehog 2* rightly enjoyed remarkable sales figures, it's important to remember how near-to-the-wire its release was. More than any other Mega Drive Sonic, its development was characterised by stops and starts. The Sonic fan community has been discovering unfinished beta versions for years, the most famous of which includes a nearly-complete additional level, the Hidden Palace Zone.

It was the stormy experience of building the game that would lead Yuji Naka and Hirokazu Yasuhara to demand major changes to the structure of the US-based Sonic Team before they undertook development of the hedgehog's next adventure.

A slightly different approach was taken for the 8-bit versions of the second game. The product developed by Japanese studio Aspect was obviously an entirely different title from its 16-bit namesake. The plot involved Robotnik having kidnapped Tails, explaining the fact that the fox wasn't present in the action, and Sonic is charged with collecting the Chaos Emeralds in order to rescue his sidekick. In theory, the game is a 'fixed' version of the first Master System release, with its engine rebuilt to allow the character to move at greater speed. Aware that it is unable to offer the blistering thrills of its namesake, the game goes to town on mid-level gimmicks, with Sonic using hang- gliders and mine carts in his bid to rescue Tails.

Even minor niggles had been addressed, with the previous game's Sonic sprite corrected to be a deeper blue, and his trainers now red instead of brown. This good work is unfortunately undone by an extremely high difficulty level, which presumably stemmed from a truncated development period, and some horrid art direction. The game's style lacks crispness, with the re-used sharp main sprite contrasting with the muddy and insipid zones he visits. You can already see the beginnings of the too-surreal level concepts which would characterise Aspect's later 8-bit Sonic games.

In the rush to capitalise on the success of *Sonic The Hedgehog*, there was a noticeable lack of coordination between the various Sega development teams. As we saw in the previous chapter, the character of Metal Sonic was a key element of *Sonic The Hedgehog CD*, yet the 16-bit and 8-bit versions of *Sonic The Hedgehog 2* both featured rival takes on the idea of a robotic Sonic doppelgänger.

The climax of the Mega Drive game had the player facing a statuesque stone-like behemoth on board the Death Egg, while on the 8-bit Sega machines, the penultimate boss of the games was the more agile Silver Sonic. Neither robot's looks had the flair of Kazuyuki Hoshino's stylish Metal Sonic design, and it's strange that these variations on the same theme would be tolerated.

This early period is one of the most interesting in terms of creative control of the franchise. With the first game, Sega of Japan effectively offered the character to its subsidiaries to market as they saw fit, taking account of the nature of their territory. Although some ideas occurred independently to all three firms involved, such as Sonic's Power Sneakers having a friction-reducing function to stop the character setting his feet alight, these notions were the exception. The results produced some interesting quirks, such as the Robotnik/Eggman discrepancy.

Sonic Team named its recurring villain Doctor Eggman, but the company's western arms felt that a more sinister moniker would have greater appeal. The character was therefore dubbed Robotnik for the (earlier) European and US releases of the game. Despite this, the scientist's egg fixation was retained in much of his additional-fiction dialogue. Sega Europe was free to construct its own conception of the character, formalised in the pseudo-factual paperback *Stay Sonic.* This utilised much guidance material which the subsidiary created for use by its merchandising partners.

The attitude towards 'origin stories' for ongoing fictional characters is an interesting cultural dichotomy between western and Asian nations. It's hard to think of any superhero from American or European comic books that isn't defined by how they obtained their powers, but the Japanese tend to give little attention to this aspect, being more interested in the finished article. Sonic Team felt no need to furnish its character with a back-story, being content just to present the hedgehog's adventures as a fait accompli.

Sega Europe, on the other hand, crafted a detailed tale that not only explained why Sonic is blue rather than the brown normal for his species, but the driving factor behind Robotnik's insanity and even reasons why the pair's world is covered in gold rings. The tale of Dr Ovi Kintobor and his ill-fated bid to rid the planet Mobius of all evil formed the bulk of *Stay Sonic.* The book was rounded out with tips on both incarnations of *Sonic The Hedgehog 2,* together with shorter chapters analysing the games' various badniks and dealing with matters such as how Sonic first met Tails.

The most striking feature of this European conception of Sonic is its literality, taking the world presented in the games as gospel in the absence of creative input from the character's creators. It was a sensible approach, perfectly chiming with the views of the games' younger players. The European Sonic mythos gave its additional fiction writers much material to work with, and remains fondly remembered.

The crowning glory of this continuity came in prose form. A total of four novels were released by Virgin publishing, all running to about two hundred pages, from a collective of three writers; James Wallis, Carl Sargent and Marc Gascoigne. Published under the pseudonym Martin Adams, they're best thought of as young adult books rather than children's titles, mainly due to the complexity of plotting and a tendency to over-reach in terms of content. For example, one book features a vividly-described passage in which Sonic spin-attacks a zombie chicken. Expecting that his opponent would be revealed to be a robot, he's somewhat nonplussed by the shower of offal which results.

The books are the most faithful adaptation of the Mega Drive games imaginable, taking the architecture of the titles entirely literally. This means that the planet Mobius is actually split into zones, in the same way that the UK is made up of counties, which can only be traversed at certain key points. Unlike the Sonic Team's conception of Sonic, the character is resolutely not a drifter, and his main motivation in each of the books is to save his friends. These are drawn from the list of names for the animals that populate the games, as furnished by Sega Europe. The only original addition to the cast of good guys is Mickey the Monkey, a dodgy cockney engineer. His role in the stories interestingly foreshadows the 1998 reinvention of Tails as a techno genius, rather than simply Sonic's biggest fan.

In what would become an established trope, Robotnik gains a robot sidekick, although Eggor's true nature turns out to be a plot point of one of the books. Speaking of the mad scientist, Adams's take on the character is truly magnificent, managing to entertain through incompetence without ever losing his capacity to create menace.

Aside from the first book, which focused solely on Robotnik's development of a new weapon, the novels each took a sci-fi staple as their inspiration. They consisted of a refreshingly complex time-travel tale, a cyberspace adventure and a horror epic that follows Robotnik's branching out into genetic engineering. At the time, the quality of the books was unprecedented, and even now they mount a reasonable claim for the title of the best piece of Sonic additional fiction. Although they don't provide a high concept for the character, their selfless adherence to the tropes of the games remains charming.

Adams always judges exactly the right moment to break the fourth wall, usually by having Sonic wryly commenting on proceedings. The writers' ability to take each of the simple tropes they borrow and make them fit perfectly into the European Sonic-verse is magnificent, and if you have even a passing fondness for the early-nineties version of the character, it's worth tracking down second-hand copies online.

Also from the same stable came a series of 'choose-your-own-adventure' books, which sadly lacked the wit of their conventional prose siblings. You can't fault the accurate reconstructions of the first two Mega Drive titles' world, but there isn't the sense of mischief that makes the novels such a joy to read. The earlier releases are probably the best of the bunch, with the second book containing an impressively complex pen & paper simulation of the video games' mechanics.

Later books such as *The Zone Zapper* and *Sonic Vs Zonik* (yet another spin on the Metal Sonic concept) are faithful to the ethos of the series, but don't make much of an original contribution. A third range of European prose books was published by Ladybird, targeted at younger children, with *Sonic The Story* being another paraphrasing of the concepts from *Stay Sonic*.

But books weren't the only way in which Sonic was able to escape the confines of video game cartridges. . .

3. Running Wild

With Sonic now established as a gaming phenomenon, it came as no surprise to find that the rights to produce a TV series based on the character were snapped up. The offering that emerged from US/French firm DiC, however, wasn't quite what was expected. *The Adventures of Sonic the Hedgehog* is best thought of as a series featuring the character, rather than one about him.

The distinctly madcap scenario pits a nomadic Sonic and Tails against Robotnik and his two minions. These additional characters were the robots Grounder (loosely based on a *Sonic The Hedgehog 2* badnik of the same name) and Scratch (loosely based on. . . umm. . . well. . .). Universally despised by fans, it's rather entertaining in places, although it clearly suffers from a lack of focus, being reliant on the writers coming up with a different gimmick every week to propel the characters into another dayglow odyssey.

As Sonic was still rather under-defined in the US when the series entered production, DiC had to make a number of leaps in characterisation for the then-silent hero, of which the more successful were retained in future incarnations. Sonic's addiction to chilli dogs, for example, was eventually incorporated into the games in 2008's *Sonic Unleashed.* Other innovations, such as the plot device of Sonic instantly donning various disguises to trick his enemies, were quietly kicked to death.

The show isn't completely awful, but did inflict a truly horrible redesign of Robotnik on the world, which took several years of brand management to stamp out. The scientist's features were exaggerated, giving him a conical head, and his dapper shirt and braces were replaced by a romper suit with a curious target cross motif. It suited the tone of the series, making the villain appear more comical than sinister, but proved bafflingly popular with several forms of additional fiction, and even made it into some pieces of Greg Martin's Mega Drive box art.

Back at Sega, Yuji Naka and Hirozaku Yasuhara were implementing the lessons they'd learnt from their most recent venture. Development of *Sonic The Hedgehog 3* commenced after a far-reaching adjustment of Sonic Team, with the two leaders putting together a mainly Japanese group for development of the series' next core instalment. Despite an olive branch being extended by their former employers at Sega of Japan, they turned down the chance to relocate the team from the US, although Naka has since admitted to suffering homesickness by this point. After abandoning initial experiments for a three-dimensional or isometrically-viewed title, they began development on another game with *Sonic The Hedgehog 2*'s format, with the goals of improving the depth of gameplay and design of the levels.

A key decision was to move the two player versus mode to a separate feature, eliminating a factor that had constrained the size of the levels in the second game, and enabling much more complex environments. The third game finally shook off the left-to-right linearity which had dogged previous instalments of the series, with the hedgehog now frequently having to double back on himself to make progress. The complexity of the characters' moveset was also increased to add more options for progress. The

Key Game

Sonic The Hedgehog 3

Release : 1994

Origin : USA

Global Sales : 1.79m

player was now able to make Tails fly at will, while Sonic was granted an 'insta-shield' which bestowed a split-second of invincibility.

Unfortunately, the full scope of this project would take time to realise, and sales of the Mega Drive were slowing. Development of the game was therefore split partway though, with Naka and his team ordered to get the first six levels of the title into shape for release as soon as possible. The second half of the game would be sold at a later date as special edition package.

Even after being cut in half, *Sonic The Hedgehog 3* remains a superb offering. The features listed above combine with a sensible restructuring of the power-up system to produce the most complex gameplay of the 2D titles. Before, the shield power-ups available had been a perfunctory inclusion, allowing characters to take a blow without losing their hard-earned gold rings. They were now split into fire, water and electric models. Each offered its own gimmick, such as the electricity shield attracting gold rings like a magnet.

These superficial features, however, were just the tip of the iceberg. Each also had its own secondary properties in resisting specific enemy strikes, and their use by Sonic unlocked a different attack move, such as the flame shield's horizontal fireball or the electrical shield's double-jump. Pretty much every aspect of the game was increased in complexity from its predecessor, with access to the Special Stage now moved to hidden giant rings. Star Posts offered access to optional bonus round mini-games, where power-ups could be obtained.

As with *Sonic The Hedgehog 2*, the plot of the game was careful to provide a pretext for the introduction of a new character, in this case Knuckles The Echidna. After the previous game's conclusion, Robotnik and his Death Egg had crashed onto the legendary Floating Island. The scientist had convinced Knuckles, the sole inhabitant, that Sonic was seeking the Master Emerald that powered the island's ancient machinery. The echidna's duty to his lost species therefore required him to protect his home from the hedgehog.

It's Knuckles who removes the Chaos Emeralds from Sonic at the start of the game, denying him the ability to go Super. Usually, Sonic Team models the gems' behaviour on their manga inspiration in the Dragonball Z comics, which scatter themselves after being used. The more intricate approach of *Sonic The Hedgehog 3* remains an anomalous departure.

At the time, Knuckles had the most complex motivation of the cast. The brief appearances he made in the game seemed to win him fans, with scarcity breeding value. It also gave Sonic Team the opportunity to add many of the mini-cutscenes which had proven so popular in the previous game, with the echidna having a habit of turning up to use the island's architecture against Sonic. In addition, the team chose to dramatise Sonic's movement between levels, adding to the impression of Floating Island as a coherent location.

Despite the success of Masato Nakamura's scores for the first two games, the composer had parted ways with Sega. The company found itself faced with the task of finding a new source of music for the third title in the series. The result was an ensemble of several musicians, resulting in a strong variety of pop-influenced tracks.

One of the composers had been a member of 1980s US band the Jetzons, and it became clear several years later that the rampantly popular Icecap Zone track was based on an unreleased song by the group. Another artist whose music was included went by the name of Jun Senoue, beginning what would become a career-defining association with Sonic.

The inclusion of a save game option in *Sonic The Hedgehog 3* meant that players could return to their favourite zone at will, after beating the game. Tellingly, the developers made the title's hidden level select code infinitely harder to activate, supporting the view that they had always intended it to be used by those wishing to replay a particular area after beating the game. It's noticeable that Sonic Team titles from 1996's *NiGHTS Into Dreams* onwards always featured the option to select cleared environments as a matter of course.

With the technical strengths of its engine, depth of gameplay and some wonderfully-conceptualised levels, *Sonic The Hedgehog 3* stands as the pinnacle of the 2D series, but neither reviewed or sold as well as its immediate predecessor. The public purchased less then two million copies of the game, a modest figure compared to *Sonic The Hedgehog 2*'s six million sales. This lead to a slight adjustment of the approach taken to the second half of the release, which was still in development at the Sega Technical Institute.

As might be guessed from this American focus, Sonic's impact in his native land was much more limited. In Japan, Nintendo's market dominance remained, with the SNES console continuing the success of its predecessor. In contrast to the wealth of comic and prose stories available to western fans, there were far fewer Japanese Sonic licences sought or granted. Manga anthology Shogaku Yonensei briefly published a series of Sonic strips in 1992, but these bore little resemblance to the games, telling the story of the timid hedgehog Nicky, for whom Sonic was a superhero alter-ego.

Despite its failings, the Master System incarnation of *Sonic The Hedgehog 2* had sold strongly. Development continued apace at Aspect on a third 8-bit title, known in the west as *Sonic Chaos*. A severely modified engine was created for this game, which for the first time mimicked the structure and gameplay of the core series, while allowing for the limitations of the 8-bit systems. The option to play as Tails, with a simplified version of his flight ability from *Sonic The Hedgehog 3*, was the main selling point for the title; in Japan, the game was released as *Sonic & Tails*.

Unfortunately, the technical demands made of the consoles resulted in compromises in the art, with some simplistic and garish design. The game tried to address this through its plot, which saw Robotnik using one of the Chaos Emeralds to alter the nature of reality itself. Despite this fig-leaf, the game remains extremely unappealing visually, as well as being far too easy.

From a fan perspective, the 8-bit game that followed it, *Sonic Triple Trouble* is of interest mainly for a continuity error, which stems from Knuckles' conversion to the white hat brigade in the second half of *Sonic The Hedgehog 3*. Taking the stopgap ending of the first instalment as a definitive conclusion, *Sonic Triple Trouble* includes the echidna in the trio of enemies confronting Sonic, with Robotnik and new character Nack the Weasel making up the numbers.

The latter is a curious figure, known as Fang the Sniper in Japan. The bounty hunter is recognised as a bona fide member of the Sonic ensemble, despite having only appeared in this Game Gear adventure and a 1996 arcade beat 'em up. Despite it not being financially viable to produce a Master System version of *Sonic Triple Trouble*, games continued to flow for its handheld brother.

The first out of the blocks were weak *Mario Kart*-clone racing games *Sonic Drift* 1 & 2. These were followed by a pair of spin-off puzzle-based platformers staring Tails, requiring the fox to use a variety of gadgets to defeat robots attacking South Island. A slightly less sane venture followed in the isometric *Sonic Labyrinth*. The greatest entertainment that this spin-off provided actually came from a scathing review in the magazine *Sega Pro*, written as a piece of Sonic fan-fiction.

The Game Gear's parting shot to the franchise came with one final title, *Sonic Blast*, featuring both Sonic and Knuckles as playable characters. It presented a bizarre combination of graphics in the pre-rendered style popularised by Nintendo's *Donkey Kong Country* with the art direction and slower gameplay of the first 8-bit iteration Sonic. It's hard not to be reminded of the cliché of an elderly Japanese solider emerging from a tiny island in the Pacific, unaware that the Second World War is long over. Somewhere in downtown Tokyo, there's probably still an Aspect office churning out Game Gear titles, blissfully unaware of their lack of sales. . .

4. Region-Specific

The ongoing success of Sonic made it clear to Sega of America that a more substantial conception of the character was needed, to rival the European set-up. This emerged in *The Adventures of Sonic The Hedgehog*'s successor series. The show was officially titled *Sonic The Hedgehog*, but is universally referred to by fans as 'SatAM', due to its Saturday morning transmission slot.

It's a completely different proposition to its predecessor, with a noticeable shift of tone. I hesitate to use the word 'serious' for a TV show about a talking cartoon animal, but SatAM was primarily an adventure series, compared to *The Adventures of Sonic The Hedgehog*'s pure comedy. SatAM's Sonic has joined a group of resistance fighters against Robotnik's control of Mobius, and hides out in a forest camp near the scientist's city stronghold.

It all sounds well and good, but there's a complete disconnection with both the ethos and detail of the games that soon begins to grate. Unlike the carefree character we know today, this Sonic is weighed down with responsibilities. Most of his missions see him sent to the grimy city of Robotropolis, a world away from the brightly-coloured pop-art environments found on the Mega Drive.

There's a general lack of consideration throughout. While this writer is personally flattered that the show gives Robotnik's first name as 'Julian', it doesn't bode well when even a cursory reading of one of the games' manuals would have highlighted the error. SatAM's Sonic is physically weaker than any other incarnation of the character, with his spin attack largely useless against the badniks on display here. The guerrillas are lead by one Princess Sally, reminiscent of the nightmarish aunts which PG Wodehouse employed to menace his leading men. The other original additions to the cast are equally poor, including a stereotypically cowardly Frenchman and one of the weaker entries in a long line of assistants that Robotnik has been lumbered with.

SatAM ran for two complete series, being cancelled before a third could move out of the pre-production stage. The concepts have continued to this day thanks to Archie Comics, who snapped up the licence to produce a US periodical. A monthly comic based on a child-friendly cartoon character may sound odd to British ears, but the title has been highly successful, notching up twenty years of continuous publication.

The quality and complexity of storytelling has improved over the years, with more characters from the games drafted in to mitigate the earlier conceptual errors. The book has usually been able to support a second title, in the first instance a quarterly special, before being replaced with, in turn, a Knuckles book, a spin off from the *Sonic X* cartoon and, most recently, a *Sonic Universe* title featuring secondary characters.

The Archie series had to divest itself of several original elements it had added to Sega's foundations after a lawsuit from former writer Ken Penders. In 2009, the writer began applying for copyright over various characters and stories he had created while working on the Sonic comic. Due to the loose terms of his contracts with the publisher, he was successful, and promptly issued a writ against his former employer. Sega was also dragged into the mix, with Penders alleging that one of the later handheld Sonic titles had been inspired by his work. The case was settled in 2013, with Penders walking away with rights to his creations and presumably a compensatory payment. Rather than agreeing an ongoing fee with its former employee, Archie instructed Penders' successor as writer of the comic to remove the disputed characters from future issues of the book.

During the proceedings, Penders claimed that Archie's actions were preventing him from launching a comics project featuring the various characters he created for the Knuckles spin-off comic. While following the case, I assumed that this claim was simply a bid to prove 'lost earnings' for the purposes of his lawsuit. To my surprise, the writer appeared to be serious, promptly commencing work on what can only be described as an extremely niche project. Penders' mood presumably contrasted with that of Archie's contracts department.

We'll come to the handheld title that attracted Penders' ire in Chapter Ten, but at the time of SatAM's transmission, the only game which seemed to draw on it was the Sega Technical Institute-developed *Sonic Spinball.* Sega of America in particular seemed to have high hopes for this tie-in, undertaking a degree of promotion unprecedented for such a venture. Released shortly after *Sonic The Hedgehog* 2, the game tasked Sonic with infiltrating and destroying Robotnik's new island-sized badnik production facility, which was entirely made up of pinball-like areas.

The title was the work of the American former members of Sonic Team, whose services had been deemed superfluous for the third main game. Interestingly, the game re-used some concepts from *Sonic The Hedgehog* 2's lost levels, with Toxic Caves and The Machine being repurposed from the Hidden Palace and Genocide City zones respectively.

Later converted to the 8-bit systems, the game is short but challenging, with the player sure to experience countless deaths before its four levels have been completed. The title was an evolution of the theme park zones found in earlier Sonic games, which frequently saw the hedgehog ricocheting off a variety of bumpers and flippers. It's definitely not a straight pinball game, due to the large degree of control that the player is given over Sonic when he's in flight.

All art assets and sprites were created especially for the title, being strongly influenced by the industrial SatAM aesthetic. It manages to find its own unique tone, but the overly challenging gameplay undermines strengths such as the technically impressive special stages and the superb boss music. Like many titles from this period without the involvement of Yuji Naka, it suffers from continuity problems after *Sonic The Hedgehog 3* established that Robotnik had been trapped on the Floating Island since the conclusion of *Sonic The Hedgehog 2.* For this reason, it makes most sense to consider the title as taking place between the first and second games, like *Sonic The Hedgehog CD. Sonic Spinball* is far from the worst cash-in the series has seen, but the unappealing art direction makes it unlikely to be anyone's favourite.

Across the Atlantic, the European Sonic-verse was still going all guns blazing, with the arrival of Fleetway's *Sonic The Comic.* The magazine was a fortnightly anthology book, published from 1993 to 2002, and would eventually comprise 183 issues of original content. The title was loosely modelled on UK sci-fi/fantasy mainstay *2000A.D.,* whose editor it shared. Each issue was built around a seven-page Sonic strip, supported by three or so stories based either on Sonic's supporting cast or other Sega franchises. The comic was briefly complemented by *Sonic The Poster Magazine*, with a short story printed on the reverse of a large-scale pin-up, but this proved short-lived, as was Ravette Books' collecting of the main *Sonic The Comic* storylines in paperback.

Although striving to be consistent with other UK holders of the Sonic licence, Fleetway had leeway to portray the character as it saw fit, giving its creatives a surprisingly large amount of freedom. A number of writers contributed to the title, with Nigel Kitching and Lew Stringer the book's mainstays. Their differing approaches complemented each other well, with Stringer's self-contained tales punctuating Kitching's in-depth epics. The artistic side was more varied, but Richard Elson's clean and energetic style deservedly secured him priority for the lead strip, which he drew for most of the comic's publication.

It's fascinating to look at the evolution in storytelling across the lifetime of the book. The early template of disposable standalone stories was gradually challenged by Kitching. His first strike was a loose adaptation of *Sonic The Hedgehog CD*, told over two months of publication. Other lengthy embellishments of Sega games' plots followed, before the writer felt confident of sustaining his young audience's attention through original epics.

A breakthrough moment came with a storyline featuring an army of Metal Sonics, which began in the backup Knuckles strip before concluding in the main Sonic feature. Aside from his keen grasp of the appeal of Metal Sonic, here dubbed 'Metalix', Kitching's other trademark was his radical reinterpretation of Super Sonic. In place of the benign demigod whom Sonic Team sought to portray, Kitching and Elson graced their strips with a spiral-eyed psychopath. The comic's longest-running storyline saw him forcibly separated from his host.

After the comic had reached the five-year lifespan that Fleetway's management had envisaged for it, the company began winding the title down, replacing back-up strips with reprints and eventually axing new content altogether. For a dead licensed comic, it's enjoyed a surprisingly active afterlife, and most of its creators still work in the industry today. Bizarrely, some of the early stories were scripted by Mark Millar, better known these days for his high-profile US superhero comics. The one exception to this, however, is Kitching. The book's lead writer sadly never found another permanent home for his scripting talents, and these days works mainly as an illustrator in the children's book market.

Given that Sega of Japan's domestic business model remained arcade-focussed for much of the nineties, it's surprising that Sonic should have waited until 1993 before making an appearance in that setting. Following from an early experiment that was basically the Mega Drive *Sonic The Hedgehog* with harsh time limits on the levels, *SegaSonic The Hedgehog* was a rather curious venture, developed in the company's native land. The game was controlled with trackballs, which were used to to guide the player characters through linear levels in a bid to escape from Robotnik's fortress.

The main source of appeal was a simultaneous three-player mode, with users controlling Sonic, the bizarre Ray The Flying Squirrel (!?!?) or Mighty The Armadillo, who was dusted off from a character design abandoned by Naoto Ôshima. The game's steep learning curve limited its success, and plans to localise it for the west using designs from the SatAM TV series fell by the wayside. Despite minimal distribution outside Japan, the title wasn't completely unknown to western fans; the author can distinctly remember being disappointed by it during a visit to London's Segaworld complex.

Sticking with spin-offs, it's worth mentioning *Dr Robotnik's Mean Bean Machine*, a Mega Drive puzzle game which dwarfs the quality of virtually every other second-tier Sonic title. The game was a western release of the Japanese *Puyo Pop*. Localisation was carried out by Sega of America, who incorporated the *Adventures of Sonic The Hedgehog* version of Robotnik, and also his robot minions. At this point, Sonic merchandise was selling strongly, with several companies making a good return on their licensing deals, and the character's owner obviously wanted some of the action.

Sega's obscure Pico machine, aimed at younger children, saw two titles featuring the Sonic gang during its unsurprisingly short life, in the form of 1994's *Tails and the Music Maker* composing tool and the mini-game collection *Sonic Gameworld*. There is nothing of any interest that can be written about either of them.

The final 16-bit instalment of the Mega Drive core series arrived late in 1994, with the release of *Sonic & Knuckles*. The echidna's popularity caused Sonic Team to alter its plans for the second half of *Sonic The Hedgehog 3*. Yuji Naka promoted his newest character to fully playable status in a second campaign, set after the conclusion of Sonic's story. There was also a change in the character's appearance. Knuckles' colour was altered to a deep red appearance, in place of the pinker tone initially selected by designer Takashi Thomas Yuda. The echidna had made an impact with players in *Sonic The Hedgehog 3*, but the combination of pink skin and long dreadlocks had caused many players to assume the character was female.

Using a customised 'lock-on' cartridge, the game could be played in a number of configurations. Simply placing the mushroom-shaped cart in a Mega Drive presents a prospect similar to original *Sonic The Hedgehog*. Lacking any selectable options save for the choice of playing as Sonic or Knuckles, players work their way through their chosen avatar's levels in the usual fashion.

Key Game
Sonic & Knuckles
Release : 1994
Origin : USA
Global Sales : 1.82m

The design of the cartridge, however, allows other games to be plugged into the top. Connecting it to *Sonic The Hedgehog 3* creates the full version of that game, with Sonic having to battle his way through fourteen large zones in order to finally destroy the Death Egg. Hirokazu Yasuhara and Yuji Naka's vision for the game is fully realised, creating a title that no 2D entry in the series has come close to matching.

Knuckles' campaign took in the same locations, and his story showed him finally expunging Robotnik's leftover badniks from the Floating Island. What proved fascinating for fans was the echidna's different abilities, with a lower jump offset by his talents for climbing walls and gliding across chasms. This offered up a different mode of progression through each of the existing *Sonic The Hedgehog 3* levels. Some acts are almost entirely altered when played as the echidna, and he offered a rewardingly complex re-routing around environments players thought they knew inside out.

But the 'lock-on' technology of *Sonic & Knuckles* offered a greater sales gimmick then the original plans for *Sonic The Hedgehog 3: Special Edition*. Although the graphical styling of each Mega Drive title differs drastically, in coding terms they were actually been built on top of each other, with chunks of engine re-used each time.

This made it a relatively simple task to insert Knuckles' sprite and handling code into *Sonic The Hedgehog 2*. There was enough space in the *Sonic & Knuckles* cartridge to throw in a few bonus areas that could only be accessed using the Echidna's abilities, completing the effect. In plot terms this was nonsensical, of course, but it compensated for the fact that building the full form of *Sonic The Hedgehog 3* would cost players a total of ninety pounds.

Contrary to popular belief, there was little trouble in also making Knuckles playable in the original *Sonic The Hedgehog*, but colour pallet problems reared their head. Sorting out the visual difficulties that resulted from would have consumed a disproportionate amount of Sonic Team's time. As a result, the planned (and vaguely obscene-sounding) *Knuckles The Echidna in Sonic The Hedgehog* was junked in favour of a hidden *Get Blue Spheres* minigame, accessed when the lock-on device was attached to Sonic Team's first title. This gave players access to a near-infinite number of layouts for the *Sonic The Hedgehog 3* special stage, which saw Sonic traversing a small globe, collecting coloured balls.

Turning back to the core title itself, *Sonic & Knuckles* effectively offered five new full-sized levels for *Sonic The Hedgehog 3*, plus an array of smaller stages designed to advance the story. Retaining the faster and expanded level schemas from *Sonic The Hedgehog 2*, Yasuhara's new assistant Takashi Iizuka ensured that a greater number of unique zone gimmicks made each location feel like an identifiable and distinct place.

The plot is choreographed in more detail than before, with several cut scenes in the Hidden Palace Zone driving forward the story. (The name is the only element in common with the scrapped *Sonic The Hedgehog 2* level.) Here, Knuckles discovers Robotnik's true nature when he seizes the Master Emerald to fuel the Death Egg, and begins to assist Sonic in his battles.

The game delved further into the mythology of the Chaos Emeralds, suggesting that they had originally been created by Knuckles' lost race of echidnas, working with the Master Emerald to power the Floating Island. The hypothesis was later revised by 1998's *Sonic Adventure*, however, which showed the Master Emerald's operation as being disrupted by the presence of its little brothers. This restored the

Chaos Emeralds' unknown origins.

The greater length of the game resulted in a risk of players having access to Super Sonic for the majority of their playthough, so the public was invited to gamble. Accessing a special stage after clearing the first six zones would bring them to the Hidden Palace's emerald chamber, where they could trade in the Chaos Emeralds, depriving themselves of Super powers, to access the next batch of social stages. Working their way through these further bonus levels would charge up the crystals into Super Emeralds, giving access to new 'Hyper' versions of Sonic and his friends, with even greater abilities.

The game's background music unsurprisingly maintained the tone from *Sonic The Hedgehog 3*, although a number of interesting changes are made to the earlier game via the lock-on cartridge. Unsurprisingly, the *Sonic & Knuckles* theme is played to signify invincibility, but there's a genuine artistic decision in replacing the short, punchy Knuckles theme with a more elaborate oriental composition. The mid-boss music, inspired by *Sonic The Hedgehog 3*'s Knuckles theme, is also removed, but the tune that replaces it was already present in the *Sonic The Hedgehog 3* code. In the vanilla *Sonic The Hedgehog 3*, the revised boss music can be heard by exploiting a glitch. Clearly the soundscape and tone of *Sonic The Hedgehog 3* was still a work in progress when the first half of the game was rushed into the shops.

While there had previously been a couple of mini-album CDs of music inspired by the Sonic games, *Sonic & Knuckles* was the first to receive a genuine soundtrack release. Although apparently recorded from the Mega Drive's sound chip, the versions of each track on the album contain movements and phrases not found in the console game's versions, having been exorcised due to cartridge memory restrictions.

The Sky Sanctuary Zone features both Sonic and Knuckles facing off against an armoured Sonic-shaped badnik. Dubbed 'Mecha Sonic' by fans, you'll recall from Chapter Two that this is actually the fourth iteration of the robot Sonic concept. The mystery was why Sonic Team hadn't revived the overwhelming popular Metal Sonic. There's no plot reason why it shouldn't be this existing character that is beaten by Sonic and then comprehensively taken apart by Knuckles.

Despite the involvement of Naoto Ôshima in *Sonic The Hedgehog CD*, it's possible Sonic Team didn't view the game produced by a separate group as canon, and wanted to try its hand at introducing its own version of the character. If this supposition is true, then at least they threw in the towel with good grace afterwards. As an in-joke in the later *Sonic Adventure*, both the *Sonic The Hedgehog CD* and *Sonic & Knuckles* robots can be glimpsed side-by-side in stasis pods in Robotnik's base. Since this point, only the popular Kazuyuki Hoshino Metal Sonic design has appeared in the series.

Perversely, the shorter *Sonic & Knuckles* attracted more favourable reviews than *Sonic The Hedgehog 3*, with the novelty of the lock-on cartridge appealing to critics. And for actual quality? It's more *Sonic The Hedgehog 3*, as simple as that. When the game is combined with its predecessor, *Sonic 3 & Knuckles* stands as a pinnacle of 2D platforming, offering an unforgettable series of environments with varied & enormously entertaining gameplay.

It also marks the end of the first stage in the character's life. From an untried venture from three eccentric designers, Sonic had powered Sega to being a genuine force in the console business. The central pillar of Sonic Team's constantly improving work was supplemented by a large array of sometimes entertaining cash-in efforts which bulked up Sega's release schedules. A considerable volume of additional fiction was available to fans keen to tie up every loose end in their hero's life.

This was all to change, however. After working on games featuring a blue hedgehog for five years, Yuji Naka and his colleagues decided that it was time for Sonic Team to begin afresh with a new concept, and relocated their organisation back to Japan. Without their guiding influence, Sonic's momentum would be considerably reduced.

The Sega Saturn Years

(1996 – 1997)

5. Dead Ends

Despite considerable marketing efforts, Sonic had never enjoyed the same degree of success in his homeland as he had in the west. When Sega of Japan faced the task of launching its 32-bit Saturn console, the firm felt it had the obvious flagship title; a conversion of arcade smash hit *Virtua Fighter*. But if the Japanese mothership was content to move its focus away from Sonic, Sega's western arms were not ready to retire the character that had served them so lucratively. With Sonic Team now wholly occupied developing a new Saturn action title, *NiGHTS Into Dreams*, Sega's subsidiaries sought help from a variety of sources to keep revenue flowing in from the aging Mega Drive, and to promote the new Saturn.

Two years after *Sonic & Knuckles*, the hedgehog made his final appearance on the console that had spawned him, in a title created by British developer Traveller's Tales. Better known these days for its successful family-orientated Lego action games, Jon Burton's Cheshire-based codehouse was approached by Sega to produce a Sonic title for Christmas 1996, the last year that the Mega Drive was commercially viable. The game was released under a variety of names, being known as *Sonic 3D: Flickies Island* in the UK. The design evolved from a rejected idea for *Sonic The Hedgehog 3*, with the playfield viewed isometrically.

The released version of *Sonic 3D* departed sharply from the usual linear levels. The hedgehog had to rescue five birds trapped inside the level's badniks, and lead them to safety, before he can clear each act. The winged creatures in the series had always been dubbed 'Flicky', in a homage to an eighties arcade title, but now that title's mother-hen concept was patched into the gameplay wholesale. Sonic's quest was to free the extra-dimensional birds from Robotnik's clutches.

The game's level structure was similar to earlier titles; each zone was made up of two acts and a boss, with special stages accessible on payment of a fifty-ring tariff.

The exploration and creature-guiding were a necessary compensation for the loss of speed and the imprecise controls arising from the isometric view. Traveller's Tales' technical know-how was not open to question, but its design work failed to reach the same standards. *Sonic 3D* is slow and fiddly to play, feeling like an also-ran.

There's a cast-iron way of distinguishing between a bona-fide Sonic game, with imagination and creative intent behind it, from a tie-in knocked out to make a quick buck. Surprisingly, this distinction pays no heed of overall quality; as stated in the introduction, development of a Sonic title is rarely more than a couple of decisions away from disaster. Many talented and dedicated individuals have put their names to games which were slated by the critics and spurned by the public.

The key is in the setting of levels, and the amount of thought that has been put into them. Given that Sonic games are all about moving through interesting places in an interesting way, it's essential that the games avoid two traps in their selection of zones. The first is simply adhering to the generic levels found in a clichéd platform game: fire area, ice area, etc. The other pitfall is rehashing the archetypal perception of a Sonic title, by opening with a tropical paradise and moving through a pinball-like area, a flying fortress and the other iterations of ideas featured in Sonic Team's first three titles.

This is best demonstrated by looking at the occasions when the Sonic Team itself returned to old ideas, as it's noticeable that the team always manage to add a new spin to the existing concept. The Flying Battery Zone shown in *Sonic & Knuckles* is a faster-paced, more high-tech setting than the similar Wing Fortress Zone which concluded *Sonic The Hedgehog 2*. The Emerald Coast stage which opens the Dreamcast's *Sonic Adventure* is a much more commercially developed area than the idyllic tropical paradise of its inspiration, *Sonic The Hedgehog 2*'s Emerald Hill. Even the most regressive title to be produced on Yuji Naka's watch, 2004's *Sonic Heroes*, added in at least one wholly novel level concept, in the form of Hang Castle.

Looking at the high-prolife 16-bit Sonic platform games not developed by Sonic Team, *Sonic The Hedgehog CD* passes this test, bringing something new to the party, whatever other design failings it possessed. *Sonic 3D* falls back on the already-tired old standbys, and so offers little to the player.

The US's Sega Technical Institute was not finished with Sonic, despite no longer being home to Yuji Naka's band of coders. Internal experiments with the *Sonic The Hedgehog 2*'s engine included code for a virtual elastic band that would tie Sonic and Tails together, enabling all sorts of slingshot mechanics. The tech demo nicknamed both *Sonic Crackers* and *Sonic Stadium* was greenlit for development as a full-blown Mega Drive game, but its development was far from smooth.

The title was quickly switched to the Mega 32X, an add-on for the 16-bit system which fixed a cut-down version of the Saturn's processors to the aging Mega Drive. The idea was to prop up the commercial chances of this ailing bolt-on, and several members of staff from *Sonic The Hedgehog CD* were drafted in to assist with development of the game.

It soon became obvious that the Mega 32X hardware was beyond help, and its existence was simply diverting Sega's resources from the Saturn, which faced stiff competition from Sony's Playstation console. The rubber stamp of Sonic's presence was pulled from the 32X game, which then received the title of *Knuckles' Chaotix*. The plot involved Dr Robotnik's attack on a theme park, which left its defenders imprisoned in a giant claw machine. Only one of the team could be released at a time, via "link ring" technology. Before tacking each act, Knuckles may swap his partner, or even surrender himself in order to allow two of his friends their freedom at once.

The cast was drawn from an array of unlikely sources. Vector The Crocodile had been intended for inclusion in Sonic's first game, but was dropped when Naka and his colleagues decided to focus on one hero alone. Resurrected as the leader of Chaotix, he was joined by custom-created characters Epsio The Chameleon and Charmy Bee. Further adding to the numbers was Mighty The Armadillo, fresh from his turn in the *SegaSonic The Hedgehog* trackball arcade game.

The game is made up of five themed zones within the park, each of which is broken down into five acts. In a break with tradition, these levels are tackled in any order, with the next act chosen from a semi-random selection machine located in the game's hub area. The levels are extremely atmospheric, with the flat-out roller coaster Speed Slider a clear inspiration for the later Sonic games' "highway" stages. The least remarkable zone, Amazing Arena, was enlivened by a gimmick whereby Knuckles would have to locate and destroy a particular machine somewhere in the level before he could cross the finish line. This touch, reminiscent of *Sonic The*

Hedgehog CD, made the common origins of the titles clear. Boss design is a little weak overall, aside from a nightmarish cross between Metal Sonic and Geiger's *Alien* design which concludes the action.

The pastel art direction is a curious choice, possibly a deliberate reversal of the garish colours in *Sonic The Hedgehog CD*. There's a richness of detail here that goes beyond any other 2D Sonic game, and some areas are remarkably memorable. Sound design is good, with appropriate and striking music. The game is actually much faster than the Mega Drive's 2D Sonic titles, with the elastic serving as a means of rapid acceleration above and beyond the classic spin dash. Several "throw" moves prevent the supporting character being stuck behind a part of the scenery.

A particular highlight of the game is its special stages. Although not winning any awards for originality, with *Sonic The Hedgehog 3*'s blue spheres added to a hexagonal tube, the 32X's 3D abilities allowed a considerable improvement on *Sonic The Hedgehog 2*'s sprite-based half-pipe. The tube often opens out into a true landscape, and the implementation of gravity physics makes falling off a real threat. *Knuckles' Chaotix* was a solid title, but its 32X home appeared to condem it to obscurity, until *Sonic Heroes*' need for a bulked-up cast saw its stars given an unlikely second chance in 2004.

The product that arose from *Sonic Crackers* was not the only title which the Sega Technical Institute was working on, although *Sonic Mars* had an even rockier ride than its sister game. The title was unceremoniously removed from its 32X host platform by Sega of America boss Bernie Stolar, and repurposed in a bid to give the Saturn a high-profile Sonic title to spearhead its second Christmas on the market. A series of poor decisions in designing the 32-bit console had resulted in Sega's machine being significantly outsold by the cheaper Playstation. Sony's system was better suited to generating 'polygon' virtual assets, which were becoming the default method of rendering graphics. Stolar was convinced that the lack of a Sonic game was a key factor in the Saturn's fading fortunes, and sought to rectify this.

Sonic X-treme, as it was rebranded, was not a 3D platform game as the term would be understood today. The mechanics of the title are best understood through comparison with one of the Saturn's launch games: has anyone played *Bug!*?

Just myself, then.

Bug! was released as part of the Saturn's first wave of software, and seemed to point the way forward for the platforming genre that had proved so popular on 16-bit consoles. Unlike how we think of a 3D adventure title today, *Bug!* followed a more limited premise, being a 2D platformer, with a twist.

Holding "up" on the directional-pad no longer caused the lead character to stare at the sky. Instead, they would walk into the screen along a narrow path, effectively adding a second plane of 2D platforming to the title, instead of a true 3D experience. The effect was achieved using a combination of 3D polygons for the levels and 2D sprites for the player and the enemies. Obviously, the dynamic camera angles we know today were impossible under this set-up.

Ironically, Sonic had made a cameo appearance in one of *Bug!*'s bonus levels, racing against the insect to pick up power-ups before dashing off at speed. It's something of a tribute to the *Sonic The Hedgehog 3* sprite that it could be inserted into a next-generation title without looking out of place. As many readers may be aware, the *Bug!*-but-faster *Sonic X-treme* never made it to market, due to the limitations of both Sega of America's resources and the console it was being built for. What we know of the title is an intriguing mix of fan-pleasing decisions and elements that sound much more eccentric.

The art direction is rather odd, with the checkerboard motif that the Mega Drive applied to zone walls taken to its logical conclusion as a subtle texture on the floor. Creatively, *Sonic X-treme* has a lot in common with the Archie universe. The plot outline feels very much in the US conception of the character, with a distinguished researcher being targeted by Dr Robotnik, keen to steal his work.

The researcher calls in Sonic to help in the struggle against the mad scientist, and the hedgehog teams up with the scientist's young niece to defeat Robotnik. There are a few touches which endear the project to fans; most noticeably the use of the distinctive American 'Sonic The Hedgehog' logo, and an early screenshot showing the inclusion of the Metal Sonic as one of the game's bosses.

For much of 1996, the in-development game was marketed as being Sega's answer to Mario 64, the true 3D platforming game that provided a demonstration of the new Nintendo 64 console's technical superiority over the Saturn and Playstation.

Sonic X-treme was well-received at the crucial Los Angeles E3 trade show, with much interest attracted by the numerous gameplay features implemented to overcome *Bug*'s problems. The screen was deliberately distorted by a 'Reflex Lens' fisheye perspective. This improved the player's peripheral vision, allowing them to see further to Sonic's left and right than a flat display would permit.

Other additions feel like more uncomfortable compromises, such as giving Sonic the ability to fire rings at enemies. This was an early recognition of the problems in depth perception when using the hedgehog's traditional jumping spin attack in a 3D environment.

Throughout the summer of that year, however, rumours about the poor health of the title began to circulate. All divisions of Sega became keener to talk about the Mega Drive's *Sonic 3D*, and the Saturn marketing campaign noticeably focussed on Sonic Team's blockbuster *NiGHTS Into Dreams*. The inevitable happened in October, when it was announced that Sonic's glorious 32-bit debut was being placed on hold indefinitely.

The impression at the time was that *Sonic X-treme* was cancelled on the orders of Sega Japan, who were unhappy with the project creatively. This is partially true, but the initial loss of momentum was due to internal problems at Sega of America. The production process placed an unprecedented level of stress on the lead programmer for the title, Chris Coffin. The coder had written the game's 3D engine single-handedly, and had been living in his office for months before the game entered the focussed 'crunch' period, where the title's assets would be pulled together to form the finished product.

When the inevitable happened, and Coffin's health collapsed under the pressure, it was obvious that the game could not be completed without outside assistance. When interviewed by fansite Sonic Cult, producer Mike Wallis recounted how Bernie Stolar had asked if anything could be done to allow work to continue. After Wallis speculated on use of the sophisticated *NiGHTS Into Dreams* 3D game engine, a couple of days later the complete source code for Sonic Team's masterpiece duly arrived from Japan. It's at this point that the politics start to play a part, and one week later Wallis was told to halt use of the engine and return the assets.

Yuji Naka himself, now moving through the ranks of Sega's senior management, was the source of this instruction. Despite his increasing desire to take full control of his creation, he'd been civil to the *Sonic X-treme* team during a visit to the US earlier in the year. The appropriation of his *NiGHTS Into Dreams* technology, however, was the straw that broke the camel's back. Sonic's 32-bit epic was dead in the water.

6. Punching. Kicking & Screaming

The principal weakness of the Saturn console was its immensely complex internal architecture, with a total of eight processors working together to run code. The machine was designed in the expectation that the 2D sprite-based graphics of the 8-bit and 16-bit hardware generations would continue to be the primary method of displaying games. The competition had other ideas, however, and Sony's Playstation was specifically constructed to render 3D polygons. With Sony's technical demos receiving a rapturous reception at trade shows, Sega attempted to boost the Saturn's 3D capabilities. Despite these eleventh hour efforts, the Sega machine was always more at home working on a flat plane than in three dimensions.

The Saturn sold a respectable number of consoles in its native Japan, where 2D games remained popular, but struggled in the west. By autumn 1996, Sega of Japan had come round to agreeing with Bernie Stolar; the absence of the company's mascot from Saturn during the first year its life had hurt it. Just as Sonic had always been more popular in the west, the Saturn's flagship series *Virtua Fighter* remained an eastern phenomenon. While the technical brilliance of AM2's fighting game effortlessly captured Japanese arcades, it was the Playstation's hovership racing game *Wipeout* which defined 32-bit consoles in Europe.

Courting both Japanese and Western markets simultaneously was essential if the Saturn was to have any hope of recovery. It was decided to restore Sonic to prominence, with control of the character abruptly removed from the American and European arms of Sega. The termination of *Sonic X-Treme* was the first outward sign of this, but it was soon complemented by a plethora of initiatives, as Sega of Japan metabolised Sonic into its development environment.

The first of Sega Japan's new wave of titles had a haphazard origin. One of the programmers behind the AM2's secondary beat 'em up, *Fighting Vipers*, undertook a lunchtime project of coding Sonic into the game. When Yu Suzuki, the head of the studio, saw the gag, he promptly pitched a full-blown title to his former subordinate Yuji Naka. Now the undisputed leader of Sonic Team, Naka was doubtful that the hedgehog's physique would make fisticuffs feasible, but he gave his approval to the project. The result was the arcade game *Sonic The Fighters*, known as *Sonic Championship* in the west. As might be expected, the title was largely modelled on *Fighting Vipers'* gameplay, with a cast of characters battling for the chance to pilot the one-man rocket ship Tails had created to assault the orbital Death Egg II.

Backgrounds for the game's arenas were in some instances inspired by memorable Sonic levels, while others were new, if not particularly original. The developers fulfilled what they saw as the duty of those working on the Sonic franchise to introduce new characters, including a wrestling polar bear named Bark, and Bean, a bomb-dropping duck inspired by a previous Sega arcade game. Although Bean & Bark failed to stick, being ignored by Sonic Team and others, AM2 did manage to make at least one contribution to the Sonic-verse. They kitted Amy Rose out with a Piko Piko squeaky mallet, which has since become her trademark weapon.

Mako Morrow's soundtrack is an odd beast. While it's tempting to describe the sound direction as wacky and comedic, due to the choice of instruments, the actual music itself is tight and controlled. Interestingly, Morrow's nerve seems to fail him when it comes to composing themes for the series' main characters. Bland compositions for Sonic, Tails and Knuckles are at odds with the wonderful piece that accompanies Metal Sonic's appearance and striking tracks for Bean & Bark. As was becoming standard, the music was given a CD release, with a bonus track included in the form of the fantastic unused piece 'Sunset Town'.

Sonic The Fighters could easily have served a role in building the character's Japanese popularity, reintroducing him to the fighting-game dominated territory. Sega's senior management, however, were extremely cautious about showing Sonic participating in violence, and the title received an extremely small arcade release. A planned home conversion to the Saturn was scrapped, ostensibly due to a shortage of programming resources within Sega.

A similarly tentative effort is found in Sega's green-lighting a Sonic anime production, which made it to market in Japan during the middle of 1996. Two half-hour episodes of *Sonic The Hedgehog* were released on VHS tapes, with an animation style inspired by the much-praised introduction to *Sonic The Hedgehog CD*. Unlike *Sonic The Fighters*, this venture underperformed due to public indifference rather than managerial timidity, and no further episodes of the show were produced.

This is unfortunate, as it was clearly a cut above the two previous American TV series. Its quality shines through in the action sequences, where a crucial balance is struck in moving Sonic's powers into a dramatic setting. A key moment is the climax of episode one, in which Sonic & Tails use the Tornado bi-plane to take down a large robot inspired by Robotnik's battle suit at the end of the Mega Drive *Sonic The Hedgehog 2*. Sonic's abilities are neither exaggerated nor underplayed, and the way in which he eventually defeats the robot feels logical and coherent.

In terms of cast, the films see Sonic, Tails and Knuckles (inexplicably wearing an Australian hat) facing off against Robotnik. A handful of human characters created for the series bulk up the numbers. In the second episode, Metal Sonic has a symbiotic link to his flesh and blood counterpart. He eventually chooses to kill himself at the close of the story, rather than continue leaching life from the real Sonic. The whole affair is of similar complexity to a multi-part *Sonic The Comic* tale.

The episodes made it to the west a couple of years later as *Sonic The Hedgehog: The Movie*, with a few cuts made. The removal of several sexual references is unsurprising, but the US & PAL versions of the mini-series also lack a moment when Sonic swears at Robotnik. It's hard to put this down to cultural differences; Sega of Japan was genuinely relaxed about its mascot expressing himself more forcefully than is normal for a Saturday-morning cartoon star.

When the planned Saturn debut of Sonic was cancelled in October 1996, Sega's Japanese arm moved fast. In view of its new-found resolve to have Sonic gain a visible presence on its struggling console, a contingency plan was implemented. When creating the 16-bit *Sonic 3D*, Traveller's Tales had been instructed to create higher quality versions of the game map renders, with a view to a future Saturn version of the title. Once *Sonic X-Treme*'s cancellation was official, Sega of Japan ordered full speed ahead on the conversion, believing that any Sonic was better than none. The release of a smartened up Saturn *Sonic 3D* took place in early 1997. It's an intriguing example of all-hands-to-the-pump across the company, with a development period of a mere seven weeks.

The core game was pieced together by Traveller's Tales, who benefited from the Saturn's formidable 2D spite handling-abilities in pulling the code across. Bridge special stages from the Mega Drive version were unceremoniously dumped. Their replacement was a polygonal version of the half-pipe levels from *Sonic The Hedgehog 2*. These fully 3D special stages were coded by Sonic Team in Japan, and at the time offered the most impressive graphics the Saturn had produced. The console's 2D processor drew some spectacular backdrops, and true transparency were effects implemented for the first time on the system.

What's more, a change working on *NiGHTS Into Dreams* had obviously been as good as a rest for the team, as the gameplay design here is brilliant. Concepts are gradually introduced throughout each of the levels, and then steadily built upon for the final stage.

The other element of note is, as always, the soundtrack. Jun Senoue's original Mega Drive score was dropped. Despite his work on *Sonic The Hedgehog 3*, the composer wasn't yet synonymous with the character, and had departed from Sega to work on a NASCAR racing title. In his place was Sega Europe's premier composer Richard Jacques, who became an intermittent presence in the Sonic series.

Jacques' work here is intriguing. There are a couple of superb tracks, most noticeably the Gregorian-inspired piece that accompanies the Rusty Ruin area. The jazz-inspired Special Stage music is similarly magnificent. In the main, through, most of the soundtrack is less than successful. It's too obvious, too potent, being like drinking concentrated fruit cordial. Luckily, Jacques' association with the series didn't end here, and his work improved greatly once he stopped trying to pastiche the original games' music.

Despite the occasional brilliance of its soundtrack, and Sonic Team's contribution, the Saturn *Sonic 3D* inherited the gameplay failings of its Mega Drive incarnation. When launched in early 1997, it was obviously a stopgap release. The game was of more interest as indicating that Sonic Team was returning to work with its most famous creation than as a piece of software itself.

Another such sign had emerged two months earlier, with the release of the *Christmas NiGHTS* odd-on pack for *NiGHTS Into Dreams*. One of the unlockable bonuses was the option to play as Sonic in a tweaked version of the game's on-foot mode. Players collected four ideyas scattered around Spring Valley, and then did battle with the beachball opera singer boss, remodelled to resemble Robotnik.

Yuji Naka and Hirokazu Yasuhara's involvement in Sega of Japan's focus on Sonic was formalised in March 1997, with the launch of 'Project Sonic'. This was an initiative across all arms of the company to revitalise the character, cement Sonic Team's creative control and use the mascot in the fight against a dominant Sony.

The first phase occurred in the summer that year, with many Japanese publicity events and a high-profile *Sonic Jam* retro-pack release for the Saturn. This effectively reintroduced the character to the Japanese market, using the relative success of the Saturn in that territory to give him a second chance at domestic fame. Amusingly, Sega of Japan launched the obvious promotional product to tie-in with the game, and an appropriately-named fruit conserve appeared on supermarket shelves. The intention was that *Sonic Jam* would lead-in to a massive publicity drive for a new bona fide Sonic Team 3D title in late 1997 or early 1998.

The start of this plan went well, with anticipation building across the industry after *Sonic Jam* was revealed at the Tokyo Game Show. The four Mega Drive titles had been subtly re-engineered for their appearances in the compilation. Alterations such as the inclusion of the standing-start spin dash move in *Sonic The Hedgehog* were obvious, but there were also quieter additions such as redesigning several levels to make them easier.

Despite this, the main selling point of the collection was the inclusion of 'Sonic World', an experiment that Naka and his team had conducted to analyse how their creation could be made to operate in 3D. Although presented as a means for players to access the collection's bonus features, such as concept art and various short films, the significance of the feature was obvious. It was widely seen as a look ahead as to what could be expected from the unannounced future title.

Even today, it's a fascinating little piece, consisting of a small Green Hill-inspired level. Sonic World is effectively a halfway house between the 2D Sonic games and the 3D formula that would emerge in 1998's *Sonic Adventure*. A number of items which would be redesigned before that title appear in their 16-bit guises, most notably the power-up monitors and old-school restart posts instead of the more 3D-friendly restart gates. There's a look to the future in the form of Sonic's altered running pose. The hedgehog now sprints with his arms held out behind him for the first time, reflecting that the character would no longer be mainly viewed from the side.

What's missing is just as interesting. There's no homing spin attack, or its non-combat acceleration variant, suggesting that Sonic Team had not yet turned its attention to how enemies would be handled in 3D. Tails appears in the level on a looping fixed flight path, with this being the only time you'll see him carrying his hero in 3D outside of 2003's *Sonic Heroes*.

After *Sonic Jam* was completed, however, the plan started to go pear-shaped. Try as they might, Sonic Team could not get the *NiGHTS Into Dreams* engine, optimised for the jester's fixed flight paths, to deliver 3D character movement at the speed they desired. So, for the second time in a year, a contingency plan was implemented. Once again, it involved a phone call to Traveller's Tales. Recognising that a full 3D Sonic game was beyond the abilities of its present hardware, Sega decided on a change of tack.

Traveller's Tales were therefore hired to produce a polygonal racing game, themed around the hedgehog's adventures. After watching *Sonic 3D* emerge, Sonic Team had a far greater understanding of the Kent-based developer's abilities, with its technical skills dwarfing its gameplay understanding. *Sonic R* was designed in Japan and built in England, with every creative decision made in the east and then couriered as drawings or instructions to the highly-skilled programmers.

Using a game engine developed for a planned Formula One title, *Sonic R* was a rushed job, completed in just six months for release in November 1997. Bearing in mind the fate that befell *Sonic X-Treme*, Sonic Team was conservative, preferring a small amount of solid content to a more substantial, but possibly flawed, effort.

As with *Sonic 3D*, Richard Jacques was hired to provide the soundtrack, but the musician made a much stronger contribution than his compositions for the earlier title. With E3 1997 rapidly approaching and little work done on the game, Yuji Naka asked that Jacques compose a vocal track to promote the title. The resulting 'Super Sonic Racing', with vocals by TJ Davis, still stands as one of the strongest bits of music to be produced for a Sonic game, and has since appeared in the series in a number of forms. Naka was rightly impressed by the track, asked that the rest of the game be scored in a similar manner, with a vocal song for each area.

In complying with this instruction, Jacques was aware that it might be controversial, and also provided slightly re-arranged instrumental versions of each piece. The levels' background music doesn't quite match the quality of the original song, but is still of an extremely high standard. Jacques' place in the series' musical hall of fame was assured, although his preference for fully orchestrated scores caused him to be an occasional contributor, as opposed to one of the series' mainstays. His collaborator Davis appeared to have dropped off the earth after the title was released, only to unexpectedly perform *Sonic R's* soundtrack live at the Summer of Sonic convention a decade later.

Sonic R seems to punch above its weight, with the slender content fondly remembered. A prime example of the game's afterlife is found in its roster of unlockable bonus characters; robotic duplicates of the original line up. This meant an always-welcome return for the Metal Sonic design created for *Sonic The Hedgehog CD*, but also the only appearance of the nightmarish Tails Doll.

The puppet is limply suspended from a head-mounted levitation device, and is shudderingly remembered by fans, starring in several YouTube horror parodies. At the time, however, the racing game received poor reviews from critics who had been lead to expect a full 3D platform game.

In truth, the writing had been on the wall for the Saturn since mid-1997, and squandering Sonic's breakout 3D title on the hardware would have thrown good money after bad. But Naka and his team had not stopped their experiments; the first true 3D Sonic game was only twelve months from release.

The 128-bit Years

(1998 - 2005)

7. The Brief Flight of the Sega Dreamcast

It was obvious to videogame publishers and their consumers alike that Sega's Saturn was not going to recover the ground it had lost to Sony's Playstation. Moderate sales in Japan were insufficient to offset a dismal performance in the west, and the Saturn's successor was fast-tracked into production. The idea was to beat both Sony and Nintendo's next machines to market, establishing a lead over Sega's better-resourced rivals that their next-generation consoles would not easily be able to catch up.

The Dreamcast system was designed to remedy the Saturn's failings. While the 32-bit console had been conservatively designed around 2D graphics, the new system looked forward to a new era of connectively. It featured a modem for online play and also a mini-console built into each memory card.

The first Dreamcast development kits became available around the time of *Sonic Jam*'s completion, and Sonic Team migrated its work-in-progress 3D concepts to the new system. The team had grown substantially since its early incarnations at the Sega Technical Institute. Sufficient staff were now employed to continue this work while simultaneously advising Traveller's Tales on *Sonic R* and completing their final Saturn title *Burning Rangers*.

Sonic Adventure was released in December 1998, about a month after the Dreamcast's Japanese launch. Experiments and concept demos had continued for a considerable period of time, with Naka and his closest colleagues heading a hand-picked team. Once satisfied with their approach, they began development proper for a period of ten months, engaging approximately sixty Sega employees. *Sonic Adventure* was the long-awaited 3D flagship for the character, but also marked the last time that his three original creators would work with him, as Naoto Ôshima left Sega to start his own company on completion of the title.

The game constituted a competed version of the handling prototype seen in *Sonic Jam*, with addition of the homing attack that makes the hedgehog's jump-on-the-enemies attacks work in 3D. Structurally, the title was an evolution of the Mega Drive instalments, with the familiar zones now dubbed 'action stages', and accessed from a network of combat-free areas which Sonic could explore at leisure.

The most remarkable aspect of the game was the size of the levels, a clear contrast to any title seen on 32-bit hardware. During an interview shortly before the launch of the game, Naka commented that the scale of the maps he had to create was the greatest problem in the title's development. The Sonic World prototype had coped reasonably well with an environment comparable to one of *Mario 64's* levels, but its star had noticeably lacked speed.

This demonstrated the need for the vast environments that *Sonic Adventure* introduced. It was these this factor which caused the inclusion of other playable characters, so players would notice the detail that had been worked into areas which they would otherwise just speed past.

Key Game

Sonic Adventure

Release : 1998

Origin : Japan

Global Sales : 2.42m

Sonic Adventure split its story between six heroes. Each had their own perspective on events, as they were caught up in Robotnik's bid to revive the ancient water elemental Chaos and use him to conquer the world. The characters' adventures crossed over at several points, with the option to start each figure's story being unlocked after the player had 'met' that hero in the game. A degree of thought had gone into this approach, with cut-scenes' dialogue experienced by more than one character varying fractionally, as if each hero viewed it from a different perspective. This eases repetition, and gives the impression that each protagonist remembers the events slightly differently.

For most of the supporting cast, Sonic's action stage settings are slightly repurposed. Only Amy and robot-with-a-conscience E102 have unique areas added to the environments, suiting their styles of platforming. Knuckles undertakes a semi-random treasure hunt, using his exploration-based abilities to navigate more open areas. The newcomer Big the Cat had a fishing-based minigame, while Tails drew the short straw. Flying was too challenging a mechanic for Sonic Team to fully incorporate, so the fox is limited to racing his hero through short sections of Sonic's levels.

Completing all the characters' stories unlocks the final section, in which control of Sonic is resumed for the climax. This approach to storytelling became typical for Sonic games over the next few years, infuriating those who only wished to play as the hedgehog. If you regard the other characters' takes on the action stages as bonus content, though, it's hard to begrudge the developers' wish to show off the environments they had created.

One of Naoto Ôshima's final tasks before his departure from Sonic Team was to redesign his creation, originally intended to be only viewed from the side, to suit a 3D model. The artist chose to make the hedgehog even more stylised, streamlining his figure. The innocent look of the 1991 design was replaced by a vicious grin, and the addition of green pupils to the character's eyes reflected a general increase in detail. This approach was then rolled out across the remainder of the returning characters, although more significant changes were made to Amy and Dr Robotnik.

The female hedgehog was completely redesigned, looking significantly older and given a simplified red dress in place of her over-complex *Sonic The Hedgehog CD* outfit. Ôshima's work on the mad scientist finally banished the memory of the *Adventures of Sonic The Hedgehog* design. The character was given an ornamented red coat with a slightly military air, as well as goggles to emphasise his engineering experience.

With minor tweaks, these versions of the characters would persist largely unaltered for the next fifteen years. The summer 1998 Japanese teaser campaign for the game's announcement emphasised the redesigns, using the quasi-silhouette image of the hedgehog's new eyes and sharper teeth against a black background.

The developers sought to give a distinct flavour to the game, drawing much inspiration from a fact-finding trip to South America. The results of this were clearly reflected in the design of the Mystic Ruins hub area and the Lost World penultimate action stage, while other levels supplied more realistic takes on standard Sonic tropes. Since then, many big-budget entries in the series have used a real-world-inspired location as their signature setting, and a base from which to expand out into more fantastical realms as seen on the Mega Drive.

This approach fits in very well with the emphasis the series has always placed on the levels' aesthetic design quality as a means of capturing potential players' attention. *Sonic Adventure* started a trend towards Sonic games as holiday-like experiences for their players, and this concept would continue through the core series for the next ten years. Even the parts of the *Sonic Adventure* outside of the Mayan setting hint at reality, with the crash barriers at the sides of the Speed Highway signature action stage a familiar sight to anyone with experience of Tokyo's road network.

The title established another template through the approach taken to publishing its soundtrack, which was the first to emerge with Jun Senoue in the role of sound director. A single CD containing the game's vocal songs formed the initial release, being followed a couple of months later by a two-CD set including all other tracks from the title. The former was a distinctly mixed bag, due to the tracks themselves. The main theme 'Open Your Heart' has a nostalgic appeal for those who played the game at the time of its release, but is actually one of the weaker compositions from Jun Senoue's 'Crush 40' band.

The rest of the vocal tracks are variable. Tails' theme stands up quite well, and has been revisited in instrumental form by many subsequent Sonic games, while Big The Cat's did much to sink the now-forgotten character. There's no such ambivalence around the full soundtrack release 'Digi-Logic Conversation', which is superb throughout. Senoue handled the bulk of composing duties, and the score established him as the definitive Sonic musician. Despite his preference for rock, he varies his approach where necessary, and it's impossible to imagine the game without his work.

The title's development was slightly truncated in order to release the game within a month of the Dreamcast's Japanese launch, and Sonic Team chose to continue work in the seven months available before the console's western release. Yuji Naka was keen for his Sonic Team division to be a true software developer, responsible for a wide array of titles, instead of merely a Sonic factory.

For this reason, *Sonic Adventure* director Takashi Iizuka relocated a small number of programmers to San Francisco, where he continued polishing the code with Naka advising from afar. Despite the marketing hype behind the western release, which was brought to Japan under the name of *Sonic Adventure International*, differences were minimal, save for an English language dub for the dialogue.

Unfortunately, the inclusion of English speech wasn't really worth the wait. Sonic Team had rightly regarded having its creation talking in-game as a huge step for the character, and expended considerable energy in auditioning the Japanese cast. This effort paid off, and in some cases the voice artists in question have been retained ever since.

Sega of America, in contrast, took a rather more haphazard approach. The actors were given single lines to perform, with no context whatsoever, instead of complete scripts. This lead to some predictably poor work, with Sonic's deadpan "*Tails. Look out. You're going to crash. Argh!*" a few minutes into the game passing quickly into legend. Luckily, this mistake was learned from, with subsequent titles seeing improvements in performance due to the provision of full scripts. The English voice cast proved a less permanent fixture than their Japanese counterparts, however, with replacement of artists a common event.

Yuji Naka was furious on learning that for 2000's *Sonic Shuffle* spin-off, Ryan Drummond had been engaged to play both Sonic and Knuckles, following the withdrawal of the latter's established actor. In fairness to Sega of American, many vocal artists have a huge range, but having the two story's two highest-profile heroes played by the same actor did seem an excessively economical approach, and Drummond's duties were restored to voicing Sonic only.

One result of Sonic Team's new-found creative control over the franchise was the resolution of the long-running Eggman/Robotnik discrepancy. Recognising that the Robotnik name had gained traction in the west, Sonic Team tried to reconcile the situation in *Sonic Adventure*. They made Robotnik the character's real moniker, with 'Eggman' Sonic's insulting nickname. This proved unsustainable, however, and shortly afterwards Sega bit the bullet and adopted the Eggman name in all territories. Most fans accepted the issue with a shrug of the shoulders, and Sega Europe have intermittently added "A.K.A. Dr Robotnik" to the brief biography of the character in the games' manuals.

At the beginning of 2000, there were only two surviving outliers from the plethora of rival conceptions of the hedgehog, now firmly overshadowed by Sonic Team's vision. Archie's comic book continuation of the SatAM version was still in publication, but now included designs based on the *Sonic Adventure* character models. The other was a third and final TV series from French firm DIC, a successor to *The*

Adventures Of Sonic The Hedgehog and SatAM. Commissioned by Sega's western divisions to help publicise *Sonic Adventure, Sonic Underground* is easily the weakest of DIC's output, and was cancelled before the end of its first season.

Essentially, *Sonic Underground* took the basic concept of SatAM, with Sonic the leader of a rebellion against the ruling power, and threw at it many additional concepts in the hope that some might stick. The show's version of Sonic is a deposed prince, who serves as the lead singer in a band with his two siblings, one of whom is predictably named 'Manic'. DIC veteran Jaleel White once again provided the hedgehog's voice, although entertainingly a different performer took over for sections in which he was required to sing.

Sonic Adventure proved to be the Dreamcast's highest-selling title, but Sega once again found itself outflanked by Sony. The announcement of the Playstation 2 console promised a level of performance far beyond the capabilities of any other system, and sent shockwaves through the industry. Sega quickly began to haemorrhage support from third-party software developers, eager to jump on the bandwagon of Sony's new venture. The reality of the Playstation 2 was considerably less impressive than the promises made, but consumer confidence in Sega slumped, and the company found itself fighting a rearguard action.

Despite this, Sonic Team's control on the franchisee remained tight, and there was no new sea of spin-offs to trade on the success of *Sonic Adventure.* The only new home title in the two years that followed was the curious Dreamcast venture *Sonic Shuffle.* This constituted a thinly-disguised rip off of the Mario Party virtual board games, with the *Sonic Adventure* character models pressed back into service. Despite some surprisingly intricate rules, the game was even duller than its inspiration, and deservedly sank without trace.

There had been no successor to the long-discontinued Game Gear, and the struggles of the Dreamcast led Sega to look on its competitors' handheld machines as a potential source of revenue. This first foray into third-party development bloomed in 1999, with the first release of a bespoke Sonic title on a non-Sega piece of hardware. *Sonic Pocket Adventure* was available exclusively for SNK's Neo Geo Pocket Colour, a niche player in its native Japan, with an even smaller amount of sales in the west.

It's a charming little game, although minimal original content was created. Level concepts and music are drawn entirely from *Sonic The Hedgehog 2* & *Sonic The Hedgehog 3* on the Mega Drive. Despite proudly displaying Sonic Team branding, the game was actually developed by Dimps, a Japanese collective that seeks deliberately a low profile, working mainly on others' properties. The fact that the company is owned by a number of other Japanese software houses, including Sega, may explain this.

SNK's handheld is best thought of as an augmented 8-bit system, and *Sonic Pocket Adventure* is a hybrid of the early Game Gear Sonics and their big brothers. Interestingly, the swipes from the Mega Drive's art direction sit side-by-side with post-*Sonic Adventure* features such as the 1998 resdeisgn of the hedgehog. Dimps have been responsible for the majority of handheld Sonic titles ever since.

With Sonic Team proper almost entirely engrossed in the development of Dreamcast role-playing game *Phantasy Star Online*, Yuji Naka decided to form a subsidiary to handle development of the main Sonic series. After years at the forefront of Sonic Team's games design, Takashi Iizuka was placed in charge of the new organisation, formed from the San Francisco group that completed the western version of *Sonic Adventure*.

Iizuka's outfit was given the unofficial moniker of "Sonic Team USA", although its games were only ever released under the more general Sonic Team branding. Mindful of the leap in his creation's popularity that accompanied the US-developed *Sonic The Hedgehog* 2, Naka felt that adopting a more American artistic direction would again benefit Sonic's global standing. In response to this directive, the team decided to set its sequel to *Sonic Adventure* in San Francisco, with a much more vivid style of imagery.

As with its predecessor, *Sonic Adventure 2* focussed on a new weapon that Dr Eggman had uncovered and was seeking to use against the world. Rather than the semi-mystical Chaos, the centrepiece of the plot was Shadow The Hedgehog, an artificial life form created by the Eggman's grandfather. Claiming to be bound to Eggman's wishes, the black Hedgehog instructed him to gather the Chaos Emeralds at the abandoned ARK space station which had been his birthplace.

As the game progresses, however, it emerges that Shadow is following the orders of his late creator, who went mad and decided to destroy the world. In the final battle, all characters team up in the style favoured by Nintendo, to counter the external threat of ARK's computer and the Shadow-prototype it unleashes.

Significantly, Shadow was not conceived as a recurring character, being killed off at the close of the game. The other debuting figure was Rouge the Bat, a jewel thief whose abilities mimicked Knuckles's. This was required by the game's duality design concept. The main theme of the title was a split between the forces of good and evil, with both sides having playable campaigns, giving their own perspectives on the story. The 'Hero' side was filled by the predictable trio of Sonic, Tails and Knuckles, with a cutscene-only Amy tagging along for the ride.

The "Dark" crew consisted of Shadow, Eggman and Rouge. The Knuckles/Rouge stages were custom-designed treasure hunting areas, and stand up superbly today thanks to their non-linear construction, as well as some outstanding design work in the case of Pumpkin Hill.

The Eggman/Tails levels reprise E-102's shooting sections from the first *Sonic Adventure*, with the fox aboard a transforming biplane mech-walker. For the most part these are the game's weakest element, with the concept only making good on its potential in Eggman's final level. That stage, Cosmic Wall, is distinguished by a genuine feeling of carnage as the scientist blasts his way through ARK's defences, aided by some inspired background music.

Key Game

Sonic Adventure 2

Release : 2001

Origin : USA

Global Sales : Unknown

Metacritic Review Average : 89%

Sonic Adventure 2 also makes a surprisingly large contribution to fleshing out the games' world. A structure of government is shown as based around a president, who has since made a number of appearances in the series, and the Guardian Units of Nations (GUN) is introduced. This military organisation functions as a peacekeeping force in Sonic's world, being the conventional response of society to the threat posed by Eggman and the like. Given that half the game is played from the perspective of the villains, and the initial arc of the Hero story has Sonic being pursued for Shadow's crimes, GUN's assault droids are the standard enemy faced throughout the title.

The main gameplay addition to the Sonic's action stages is 'grinding' along rails and metal beams in the style of skateboarders, highlighted through a tie-in promotion with the now-discontinued footwear brand Soap Shoes, which the hedgehog duly sported throughout the game. The grinding model in *Sonic Adventure 2* is slightly more complex than in subsequent titles, with momentum and the direction in which Sonic is leaning having an impact on his speed and progress.

This gameplay element was mainly introduced to give variety to Sonic's progression, instead of having him continually running down narrow pathways. It's been a mixed blessing for the series, providing an alternative means of movement for action stages, but also giving a lazy way for developers to increase the difficulty, by simply filling an area with split-second girder-to-girder jumps.

Takashi Iizuka was forced to develop the game in the face of Sega's growing financial difficulties, and so could not call upon the formidable level of resources marshalled for the first *Sonic Adventure*. The reduced team was not able to create bespoke and tailored environments to the same degree as the previous title, resulting in a re-use of a toolbox of elements and assets to build each stage. There are fewer open vistas compared to *Sonic Adventure*, to allow smoother animation, and it can seem at times as if the hedgehog is moving through a confined trench rather than an open world.

The brasher feel is immediately obvious, both in the vividly sun-drenched stages and Jun Senoue's more forthright soundtrack. To underline the fact that the game was a direct sequel, Senoue remixed and rerecorded returning characters' vocal songs, as well as *Sonic Adventure*'s various power-up jingles. The remainder of the soundtrack was entirely new, with Fumie Kumatani, amongst others, supporting the lead composer, and there was an attempt to give a distinct musical style to each character's stages.

Sonic Adventure 2 was released on the character's 10th birthday, the 23rd of June 2001. A limited-edition version was sold in Europe exclusively through Sega's website, including a brief history booklet, a commemorative coin and a music CD. This was a slightly cut-down version of the Japanese 'birthday pack', which also included an oversized box.

A more substantial acknowledgement of the anniversary was found on the game disk itself. Obtaining a one hundred percent completion score on the title would unlock a polygonal reproduction of *Sonic The Hedgehog*'s Green Hill Zone, carefully crafted in the *Sonic Adventure 2* engine. Another nod to the past saw a return by the two-player split-screen competition mode last seen in *Sonic The Hedgehog 3*. While this mode is known to be a favourite of Yuji Naka, it probably doesn't justify the simplification imposed on the action stages included, which had to be tailored so that the Dreamcast could render each twice.

Although *Sonic Adventure 2*'s more linear ethos meant it fell slightly short of the original game's high standards, it was still a high quality effort. Sadly, it served as the Dreamcast's obituary, being released four months after Sega announced that its last home console would be discontinued. The videogame hardware business requires companies to shoulder considerable costs as they develop their machines and spend on advertising to build up a userbase. They then hope to recoup their outlay through game sales and licence fees, in the later years of the machine's life.

With resources diminished by the truncated life of the Saturn, Sega could not sustain the short-term losses in supporting the early years of the Dreamcast's life, and so announced its withdrawal from the hardware market in March 2001. After a decade-long stint as Sega's company mascot, Sonic had outlived the consoles he was created to promote.

8. An X-Tra Life

In theory, Sega's transformation from console manufacturer to a third-party developer for others' systems should have been of benefit to the Sonic franchise. The company was being assiduously courted by the former rivals who had run it into the ground, and its studios had been freed from the schedule constraints of supporting a specific hardware platform.

The reality was more muted. Sega was perilously close to bankruptcy, and the lavish project budgets which had marked the Dreamcast era were now only a memory. Just as importantly, programmers could no longer count on receiving the latest development tools and debug units. Instead of favouritism from their hardware-development colleagues, Sega's software teams joined the long queue of firms at the doors of Sony, Nintendo and Microsoft, whose Xbox console had just entered the fray. Sonic had a clear creative direction, and a strong controlling hand from Sonic Team, but the next few years of his life would be a struggle to make good on that vision, due to financial constraints.

The first priority for Sega was to get money coming in through the door, and so *Sonic Adventure 2* was hastily re-released for Nintendo's new Gamecube system. Despite a mere six months having passed since the well-received Dreamcast version, the title received a bafflingly rocky critical response. It still managed to sell one and a half million copies at retail, an achievement given the Gamecube's limited user base, and an enhanced port of the original Sonic Adventure was put into development for the Nintendo console and PC.

After completing *Sonic Pocket Adventure*, Dimps were commissioned almost immediately to develop *Sonic Advance* for Nintendo's Gameboy Advance system. This portable title bore the greatest resemblance to the first 16-bit Sonic title, with the titular hedgehog, Tails, Knuckles or Amy having to make their way through six stages in the established 2D style. Taking possession of the Chaos Emeralds from a skyboarding special stage offered access to a final area. Bland level design and uninspired concepts gave early warning that Dimps' output would not hold the interest of those who had experienced the original 2D games. *Sonic Advance* was released in late 2001. A port to ill-fated phone/handheld-console hybrid the Nokia N-Gage followed a couple of years later, in accordance with Sega's apparent preference for systems with limited commercial prospects.

The revenue from the limited Nintendo ventures justified recommissioning Sonic Team USA for the next title in the series, *Sonic* Heroes, although a much reduced budget was available. With several years having elapsed since *Sonic Jam*, another retro pack was quickly released to consolidate the Sega's presence on the Gamecube, containing the original four Mega Drive games.

In contrast to the situation on home systems, Sega's experience of working with SNK left it fully acquainted with a third party role on mobile platforms, and Dimps was soon instructed to produce a sequel to *Sonic Advance* using the same engine. Some minor alterations were made to the gameplay to incorporate elements from *Sonic Adventure 2*, such as Sonic's use of stunt pads to launch himself into the air and an adjustment to the way the spin attack operated. For the most part, however, the 2002 title was essentially more of the same, with a similar lack of inspiration in level design.

The game was most notable for introducing a new character in the form of Cream The Rabbit, a six-year-old girl who took Amy's slot in the roster of playable characters. Cream is unique for two reasons. Firstly, she has easily the worse name in the entire Sonic canon, sounding like an instruction you'd receive when following a Heston Blumenthal recipe. Secondly, she's the only character to be shown as having a blood relation, with her prime motivation in the game being to rescue her mother, Vanilla. This doesn't sound particular striking, but given Sonic Team's reluctance to expound on its heroes' origins, it's the only indication that Sonic characters aren't simply found under gooseberry bushes.

Sonic Advance 2 again sold like hot cakes, and a third effort would eventually appear in 2004, with a character swapping gimmick inspired by *Sonic Heroes'* team-up concept. This was joined on the Nintendo handheld by *Sonic Battle*, a frankly bizarre isometric beat 'em up, as well as *Sonic Pinball Party*. Unlike *Sonic*

Spinball, there was no plot attached to this game, which simply included a pinball table themed around the Sonic series in its roster. Interest was further muted by the fact that it recycled art and sprites from Dimps' Game Boy Advance titles.

Although no fully-fledged game was released in 2003, it remains an important year for the character, due to the launch of *Sonic X* A Japanese children's cartoon series masterminded by Sonic Team, the show's premise saw the Sonic characters trapped on earth. Various misadventures then ensue as they try to adhere to their traditional modus operandi in a more real-world setting. *Sonic X* may have been the fourth in a procession of TV incarnations of the character, but it's easily the best, remaining true to the concepts of the games while creating its own unique setting.

Sega's involvement in the venture was extensive, with a soundtrack created by its Wavemaster sound studio and Yuji Naka undertaking promotional duties for the project. He explained to fans that the series did not follow the same continuity as the games, taking place in "*a different dimension*".

The highest-profile addition to the games' characters is Chris Thorndyke, a lonely rich kid who saves Sonic from drowning at the end of the opening episode. His house comes to be used as a base of operations by the forces of good. Although the boy's parents make fleeting appearances when the plot requires, Chris's eccentric inventor grandfather and the family's samurai-obsessed butler take more significant roles. It's an utterly charming little show, with perfect characterisation throughout. Although initially commissioned for thirteen episodes, approval was quickly given for a full run of twenty-six, allowing a long-running plotline regarding Eggman's accumulation of the Chaos Emeralds to play out. Although the programme isn't high drama, there's a trace of real emotion in the finale, which has Sonic and Chris both willing to sacrifice themselves to save the other.

The commercial success of *Sonic X* was tremendous, with a far greater volume of merchandise shifted than any other single iteration of the character has given rise to. After initially airing on Japan's TV Tokyo, a western dub was broadcast in the US on Fox, and then distributed through many other countries. A second run of 26 episodes was ordered, but the script team found that its originally-planned story arc was complete, and they had few places left to take the show.

This problem was partially resolved by using most of Season Two to present adaptations of the two *Sonic Adventure* games, although they suffered from the need to shoe-horn Chris into the existing plots. There's an upswing in quality for the final ten episodes, which feature original storylines. Events are further enlivened by a particularly amusing fourth-wall breaking debut for Chaotix, who have missed out of the action so far and have to catch up on events by viewing the DVD releases. The Season Two finale is effectively a reprise of the end of Season One.

In one respect, the second series of *Sonic X* performed an invaluable service to the character, providing a sustained examination of his life philosophy. In the final arc of the series, the people of the world are beginning to mimic Sonic's approach, not bothering to attend work, and spending the day lazing around until something catches their attention. It's eventually revealed that the problem is due to Super Sonic having merged two dimensions together at the close of the first series, but the spotlight it throws on the character is illuminating. It confirms that the portrayal of the character throughout the show has been no accident. Unlike Tails, who has made a home for himself in the Grandfather's workshop, Sonic has never sought a room in Chris's house, being content to sleep outside and apparently lacking any personal possessions.

This supreme reluctance to be tied down is consistent with the games, and goes a long way to explaining why the titles have seldom seen Sonic return to the location of a previous adventure. Sonic is perpetually on holiday, always moving on and finding new places to explore. He's indolent, however, rather than hedonistic, being perfectly willing to doze the afternoon away rather than engaging in an activity that doesn't interest him. He'll pursue a goal with tenacity, but remains unattached from life, appreciating the moment with little forward planning. His friends serve as his only link to the rest of the world.

Tellingly, Sonic is never shown to acquire a house or even a permanent residence in any of the games, in contrast to his supporting cast. At the start of a story, his wandering is always bringing him to somewhere new, and he reacts to what he meets there.

This distillation of his character may go some way to explaining why he's proved so resistant to taking root in Japanese culture. He's the antithesis of his home nation's work ethic and strong social identity, and a large part of the *Sonic X* message is that his actions are unsustainable in large sections of the population. The way Sonic relates to a human perspective on life, and his perpetual lack of attachment to others, would later be a key theme in the finale adventure Yuji Naka supervised for his creation.

For some regions, the definitive conclusion for *Sonic X* came at the end of Season Two, with Sonic and his friends returned to their home planet. Outside of Japan, however, there was still considerable network demand for the show, and so a further Season Three was produced. This had stronger fantasy and sci-fi elements, being set on Sonic's unnamed home world, to which the grown-up Chris has constructed a portal. Unusually, this final run of episodes never received a Japanese broadcast, despite a full dub of the series being created in that country's language. American enthusiasm for the series was also sufficient to sustain over twenty-five issues of a dedicated comic book from Archie, as well as bucketloads of action figures, cuddly toys and other merchandise.

One unfortunate consequence of *Sonic X* was the sacking of the games' English vocal cast. When *Sonic X* came to the west in 2004, localisation firm 4Kids declined to follow the example of the Japanese original series, and hire the actors who had voiced Sonic and company in-game. Instead, it preferred to use its own performers. This drew some disquiet from the Sonic fan community. Despite poor work in the first *Sonic Adventure*, Ryan "Sonic" Drummond in particular had embraced the games' followers, being more than happy to give interviews to fan websites.

What followed added insult to injury, with Sega of America then deciding to use the 4Kids performers in all games that followed. This cost-saving measure understandably lead some fans to take further umbrage against Sega of America, although the quality of performances remained largely unchanged. 4Kids actor Jason Griffith's Sonic sounded a little younger than Drummond's, but that's the only difference. *Sonic Heroes*, the next major home console game, would be Drummond's final performance as the character.

This, the second title from Sonic Team USA, had its western release in early 2004, with considerable fanfare made of its status as the first multi-format Sonic game. The title was simultaneously launched on the Playstation 2, Gamecube and Xbox. After *Sonic Adventure 2*, Takashi Iizuka and his fellow developers appear to have set their sights lower, although the constantly-tightening budgetary constraints will have played a part. While *Sonic Adventure* was the work of a sixty-strong team, *Sonic*

Heroes was produced by less than a third of that total. The game was conceived as a nostalgic look to the past of the series, with a return to the familiar checkerboard-walls art direction. This bid to appeal to a Sony-console audience, who had not touched a Sonic title since his salad days on the Mega Drive, proved successful.

Sonic Heroes passes the 'new level concepts' test outlined in Chapter Five, thanks to Giant Metropolis's pop-art futurism and the haunted Mystic Mansion, but the game is squarely conservative. There's minimal emphasis on story and greater attention paid to fixing legacy gameplay problems. The main innovation is allowing the player to control a team of three characters at once, with the primary character switched at will to allow the use of differing abilities.

These powers were modelled after the trademark abilities of the lead 'team' with Sonic giving access to high-speed platforming, Tails having limited flight abilities and Knuckles offering a wide range of combat options to fight the more heavily-armed badniks Eggman has deployed.

Other teams have to fight their way through tweaked variants of the stages for Sonic's squad. Team Dark poses the hardest challenge, lead by an amnesic Shadow. In an early cutscene, the black hedgehog is discovered to

> ## Key Game
>
> ### *Sonic Heroes*
>
> **Release :** 2003 / 2004
>
> **Origin :** USA
>
> **Global Sales :** 5 . 46m
>
> **Metacritic Review**
> **Average :** 70%

be held in suspended animation in one of Eggman's bases. He's joined by Rouge and a psychotic malfunctioning robot, E123. Clearly influenced by *Sonic Adventure*'s E102, his presence means that two thirds of Team Dark had received semi-plausible resurrections. The remainder of the action is shared between Team Rose (Amy/Cream/Big) and a revived & redesigned Chaotix (Espio/Charmy/Vector), who are now portrayed as a group of private detectives.

There's a distinctly retro tone to events, with the earth-like cities and civilisations of the previous two core games downplayed in favour of a fantasy setting in which Eggman is the only human seen. The story has an apparently ordinary offensive by the scientist revealed to be nothing of the sort, with the real Eggman held prisoner and impersonated by his upgraded Metal Sonic.

The android has freed himself from loyalty to his creator and decided to eliminate all organic life, using Eggman's arsenal to do it. In the finale, Super Sonic takes down his counterpart, who is captured and reprogrammed back into obedience by Eggman. Impressively, artist Kazuyuki Hoshino was re-engaged to supply the upgraded Metal Sonic's design, with a skirt section added to his armour for this one appearance only.

Another pleasing factor is that the game follows the classic 16-bit two acts & then a boss structure, although a last-minute change saw the acts comprising each zone being given separate names. This was probably to allow a back-of-the-box boast of fourteen levels. It's interesting to hear Jun Senoue working with a more traditional style of game, while sticking to his guns on the use of electric guitars.

The problem with *Sonic Heroes* is that Sega overreached itself in its first truly multi-format title, with the bought-in Renderware game engine producing a lacklustre mess. The handling of the characters never feels quite right, with the homing attack lacking crispness and physics frequently giving the impression that every surface has been covered in butter. While its heart is in the right place, these technical and gameplay shortcomings limit the game's appeal. It's telling that the title has since had a muted programme of digital marketplace re-releases, despite selling extremely well, particularly in the UK. *Sonic Heroes* was the hedgehog's big chance to reconnect with the mass-market audience which had eluded him since 1994, but his parent company's crippled finances had left him hopelessly under-prepared for the challenge.

9. The Sonic Cycle

The commercial success of the under-developed *Sonic Heroes* was beneficial to Sega in the short-term, but its long-term impact damaged the Sonic series. A decade on, *Sonic Heroes'* art direction has arguably supplanted the visuals provided by Naoto Ôshima as defining the franchise. When Sonic appears in a spin-off production, the depiction of his natural environment is more likely to be rooted in *Sonic Heroes'* opening stage Seaside Hill than the totem poles of the Green Hill Zone.

Sonic Heroes sold well to a mass-market welcoming the character back to mainstream consoles, but the uneven gameplay sullied their memories of the 16-bit Sonic titles. This disappointment laid the foundations for the negative opinions of the series which would come to dominate the videogame press.

Rather than seeing *Sonic Heroes* as an unlikely triumph for the bare-bones Sonic Team USA, Sega's management believed that they had struck gold, immediately putting Takashi Iizuka and his team to work on a follow-up title. As with its predecessor, this game would use the visually unappealing Renderware engine to allow simultaneous release on the three dominant consoles of the day. The main problem the game faced was disenchantment amongst its development team. *Shadow The Hedgehog*, as the project became known, was the third Sonic-related game in succession to be commissioned from the San Francisco outfit, and the prospect was viewed with considerable apathy.

Yuji Naka's fears of a Sonic-factory had been realised in the subsidiary under his control, but he could not deny Sega's pressing need for the revenue which the series brought in. As for Iizuka, he was also keen to take a break, but management showed no signs of authorising his pet project; a sequel to 1996's *NiGHTS Into Dreams*. Third-party development had not brought the expected improvement in Sega's fortunes. Early 2004 saw the company taken over by the Sammy Corporation, a Japanese supplier of gambling machines.

The ethos of the *Shadow The Hedgehog* was wholly commercial, seeking to maximise sales at almost any price. Enviously eying the success of the revitalised *Grand Theft Auto* crime comedies, Sega was minded to give its mascot a harder edge. The result saw shooting mechanics introduced into the title, with the traditional spin attack only a secondary option in combat. It was originally intended that Sonic would be the one pulling the trigger, but intervention of Yuji Naka saw his hero distanced from the experiment. As a result, Shadow was given the lead role, with the title becoming a direct sequel to *Sonic Adventure 2*.

The result is hilarious in its efforts to adopt Goth and emo trappings. *Shadow The Hedgehog* is clearly regarded as something of an embarrassment by Sega, with the game noticeably downplayed in Pix N' Love's 2012 official history of Sonic. The attempt to portray Shadow, a cartoon hedgehog, as a tormented and angst-filled presence inflicted near-fatal damage to the once-popular character.

Key Game

Shadow The Hedgehog

Release : 2005

Origin : USA

Global Sales : 1.78m

Metacritic Review Average : 48%

The principal enemy in *Shadow The Hedgehog* is Black Doom, an alien warlord, and his army of minions, the Black Arms. The game opens with Shadow, amnesic as established in *Sonic Heroes*, watching the Black Arms bombard the planet. He's soon contacted by their leader, who claims to be Shadow's true creator, and demands his assistance in subduing the earth.

The duality theme from *Sonic Adventure 2* is given a far more direct gameplay role here. In each stage, Shadow must decide whether to help the forces defending the Earth, typically a mixture of GUN troops and one of Sonic's allies, to support the Black Arms' invasion or just to follow his own interests by accumulating the Chaos Emeralds.

The game follows a branching structure similar to the eighties Sega driving title *Outrun*. The objective Shadow chooses for each level determines where he heads next and what direction the story takes. There were a considerable number of endings to the game, and the player was only granted access to the final section after sufficient alternatives had been explored. Cunningly this respected player agency while retaining the character's ambiguity.

The conclusion ties up the dangling plot threads relating to Shadow's origin. Eggman's grandfather was revealed to have struck a Faustian pact with Black Doom to gain the technology to create Shadow. The resulting guilt was what drove him to the madness seen towards the end of *Sonic Adventure 2*. Shadow eventually decides that he will not assist Black Doom, and destroys the alien forces, before accepting a permanent job as GUN's top agent.

Although built using *Sonic Heroes'* mess of an engine, the run & gun shooting gameplay doesn't suffer quite as much from the flimsy technology. The need for precision platforming is reduced, and only isolated instances of Sonic's trademark speed reduce the technical demands on the engine. Compared to its predecessor, *Shadow the Hedgehog* is a better realisation of a conceptually inferior game, although there's an undeniable air of exhaustion about the title. Several *Sonic Adventure 2* locations are revisited, but the art direction lacks the sharpness seen four years earlier.

Perhaps mercifully, the Christmas 2005 release of *Shadow The Hedgehog* was overshadowed by the launch of Microsoft's Xbox 360. With the 'bit' classification obsolete, this was the first of what came to be known the seventh generation of consoles to reach the market. Sonic Team USA's venture was supported by a more fondly-remembered handheld title from Dimps, this time on the Nintendo DS.

Sonic Rush was a distinct improvement over Dimps' releases for the Gameboy Advance. There was a stronger emphasis on plot, with an extra-dimensional invasion kicking off proceedings. The new arrivals consist of Blaze The Cat, a second playable character tackling the same levels as Sonic, and her arch-enemy Eggman Nega, politer and more sinister than his everyday counterpart.

Blaze was an instant hit with fans and press alike, with her flame-generation powers providing a different gameplay style to the hedgehog, without sacrificing his speed. On her world, she combines the roles of Sonic and Knuckles, acting as guardian to the vital Sol Emeralds. *Sonic Rush* succeeds by virtue of its striking art direction, with a memorable Greek aesthetic in some of the levels.

Attention was lavished on the game due to its very atypical hip-hop soundtrack from *Jet Set Radio* composer Hideki Naganuma. The actual level layouts remain weak, however, with the introduction of a chargeable Boost sprint move further downplaying platforming. In contrast to the main game, the half-pipe special stages feel wonderful. They made skilful use of the DS's touchscreen interface, although they were slightly too easy. As with the majority of the handheld games, *Sonic Rush* sold by the ton.

For the five years since the turn of the millennium, development of Sonic titles had been concentrated in Iizuka's San Francisco offices, and at Dimps in Osaka. The commercial drive which had guided the development of *Shadow The Hedgehog* now resulted in an attempt to add a third string to the franchise's bow. The game that resulted displayed a more competent approach to multi-format development than the output of Sonic Team USA, but unfortunately this spin-off didn't supply compelling gameplay to match. *Sonic Riders* was a spiritual sequel to *Sonic R*, putting the cast atop racing hoverboards. The plot concerned attempts by Eggman and new street gang villains The Babylon Rogues to uncover an ancient treasure.

The game was developed by the Japanese Sonic Team, but this was not the same organisation that had created 1998's *Sonic Adventure*. Gameplay designer Hirokazu Yasuhara departed from Sega in 2002 to work at Naughty Dog, an American studio owned by Sony. This left Yuji Naka as the sole representative from the trio of minds which had created 1991's *Sonic The Hedgehog*. A year later, the studio's heritage had been further diluted by an injection of staff from the dissolved Sega group United Game Artists. Although UGA had a prestigious history, creating the *Space Channel 5* series and *Rez*, it was arguably castrated by the departure of its charismatic leader, Tetsuya Mizuguchi.

Development of *Sonic Riders* was carried out by ex-UGA staff. The developers made a reasonable attempt at introducing depth, with the hoverboards having a large number of stats to tune. They failed, however, to solve the core problem of multi-route combat racing games, leaving victories too heavily dependent on chance. A bland techno soundtrack further diminishes interest, but Sega seemed to be taken aback by the failure of the venture. A sequel had already been green-lit before the release of the title, with the Nintendo Wii follow-up *Sonic Riders: Zero Gravity* eventually sinking without trace in 2008.

With development of *Shadow The Hedgehog* complete, Sonic Team USA was on the verge of mutiny. Sega's management were forced to approve production on *NiGHTS: Journey of Dreams* rather than force the team to continue working exclusively on Sonic games. Despite this, there was a pressing need to establish Sonic's presence on the seventh generation of consoles, with the already-released Xbox 360 shortly to be joined by Sony's Playstation 3.

Many of the problems that had beset Sega since 2001 had been caused by the inferiority of the company's development tools and techniques. While other third party developers had been experimenting with the quirks of the Playstation 2 since 1999, Sega only began to accumulate knowledge after the Dreamcast was discontinued. The company arguably never overcame this handicap.

With Iizuka finally working on NiGHTS, the Sonic franchise was effectively relocated back to Japan, being placed in the hands of Sonic Team proper. Development began on a custom-created multi-format game engine for the next title, and an extremely impressive technical demo was shown behind closed doors at the 2005 Tokyo Game Show. The footage had Sonic facing off against a large number of enemies, before transforming into Super Sonic and ploughing through them. With the technology coming together, Yuji Naka devised the concepts and themes for what would be his final venture with his creation.

Naka was one of the figures that who fought frantically to keep Sega afloat when it faced the threat of bankruptcy in the first part of the decade, but considered his debit to the stabilised firm paid. Having obtained financial backing from Sega to fund his planned independent developer, Prope, he devised his parting shot to Sonic carefully. His main desire was to examine the question of how his creation would fare in the real world. With the intention that the game would see the rebirth of Sonic as a key part of the new generation of consoles, the unadorned name *Sonic The Hedgehog* was chosen. Fans usually refer to the title as *Sonic '06* to distinguish it from the 1991 Mega Drive game.

The gameplay would have a similar structure to *Sonic Adventure*, although it appears that at this point, Sonic was intended to be the only playable character. The plot would mirror the 1998 classic *Sonic Adventure*, which pitted Sonic against the Chaos water elemental; this time the hedgehog would face a similar creature composed of flame. After the Mayan setting of *Sonic Adventure*, and the San Francisco styling of *Sonic Adventure 2*, this time the city of Venice served as the inspiration for the game.

The story crafted showcased both Sonic's strengths and weaknesses, demonstrating his strength and dedication, but also his refusal to accept permanent responsibilities. A key part of this was his "relationship" with Elise, the human ruler of the city-state in which the game was set. Despite the superficial trappings of romance, the plot makes clear that the deliberately cartoonish Sonic is incapable of commitment to another creature.

With the roadmap for the game established, Naka departed from Sega to take up his new role. *Sonic The Hedgehog (2006)* was gradually diverted into a more expansive venture, with the blue hedgehog being joined in the game by new character Silver and, finally, Shadow. Silver's gameplay was taken wholesale from a planned revival of a classic Sega franchise. His telekinetic abilities operated in a context-sensitive fashion, as he strived to

Key Game
Sonic The Hedgehog
Release : 2006
Origin : Japan
Global Sales : 2.07m
Metacritic Review Average : 45%

change history and prevent the apocalyptic future from which he hailed.

Despite the harder edge which Shadow retained, he only deploys vehicles, not guns, playing like a more combat-orientated version of Sonic. Interestingly, he's able to pull off in realtime the teleport tricks that were present in the introductory movie of *Shadow The Hedgehog*, but not in the actual gameplay.

Each of these three leads were joined by a pair of supporting characters, who are playable for bonus levels and short sections of the core stages. Sonic and Shadow are joined by their teammates from *Sonic Heroes*, whilst Silver has rag-tag reinforcements in the form of Blaze The Cat and Amy Rose. The implementation of these characters varies enormously. Knuckles and Amy are barely functional, but Blaze is wonderful to play as, being faster than even the star of the show. It's worth noting that the Blaze shown here is Sonic's universe's version of the character, residing in Silver's future setting, as opposed to the parallel-dimension incarnation which provided her debut on the Nintendo DS. Blaze is killed off at the end of Silver's story, but as the conclusion of the overall time-travel plot undoes the game's events, she's presumably still alive. The other big success of the game was the implementation of Tails, with the addition of ranged attacks to the character finally making his scattershot flying function effectively in 3D.

Jun Senoue was presumably lying in a darkened room after completing the soundtracks to *Sonic* Heroes and *Shadow The Hedgehog* almost single-handedly. As a result, the bulk of the game's music was handled by a team of Tomoya Ohtani, Hideaki Kobayashi and Mariko Nanba.

Ohtani would become Senoue's successor as the lead composer for the Sonic series. His tracks here are an interesting half-way house between Senoue's Sonic house style and the main-theme-driven approach which he would later develop. Game director Shun Nakamura obviously had high expectations of Kobayashi, tasking him with providing the music for the signature Kingdom Valley stage, but the result is disappointing. Kobayashi's work tended to prioritise atmosphere over a strong and recognisable tune. He'd later prove to be more adept at arranging others' scores.

The most frustrating aspect of *Sonic The Hedgehog [2006]* is that it's so very nearly wonderful. The stages are well-conceptualised, it offers a variety of gameplay styles, the story is intricate and well-crafted and the main theme tune is superb. A slight redesign of Sonic, giving him longer arms and legs, works superbly. Unfortunately, development was mismanaged following Naka's resignation, and the final product suffered numerous quality issues, with severe bugs and appalling load times.

Coding began well before Xbox 360 and Playstation 3 development kits became available, and the game was never properly converted from the advanced PC architecture that initially housed it. Pressure from both Sega (desperate for a holiday-season release), and Microsoft (who wished for the game to be on sale before the launch of Sony's new console), saw the title sent for production in an obviously-unfinished state.

In the behind-closed-doors demo of Kingdom Valley shown a year before release, Sonic moved at his usual speed, travelling at about twice the pace he managed in the finished game. It was intended to include a gameplay mechanic whereby the hedgehog would move faster as he collected more rings, but this was unceremoniously cut, leaving the hero practically crawling. What should have been a triumphant return for the *Sonic Adventure* style of game can only be played through gritted teeth.

The commercial performance of the title matched its quality, and *Sonic The Hedgehog [2006]* sold far fewer copies than *Sonic Heroes*. Grave damage was inflicted on the franchise, cementing in the minds of many video game fans the poor impression created by the Renderware titles. It's after this release that we start to see references to the 'Sonic Cycle', an internet meme in which the series promises that each new game will be a return to form, and hopes rise, only to be dashed by the quality of the final product.

With dismal review scores, Sega was forced to implement remedial actions. A candid blog post from former employee Ben Andac reported that morale within Sonic Team was at rock bottom. He alleged that semi-sweatshop conditions had disillusioned many staff, who had been trapped working on the Sonic franchise for years. New studio head Tetsu Katano pledged to improve working conditions, but faced an uphill struggle to restore Sonic's reputation.

The Seventh Generation Years

(2006 – 2012)

10. Two Years of Side-Steps

The early years of the seventh video game consoles generation were sobering times for Sega. The company had assumed that its once-prestigious titles would be welcomed with open arms by its former rivals. This initially proved to be the case, with Microsoft in particular opening its chequebook to obtain new entries in the *Panzer Dragoon* and *Jet Set Radio* series. After the launch of the Xbox 360 and Playstation 3, however, relationships cooled as Sega's fantasy influenced offerings became increasingly out-of-step with the direction of the western marketplace. Even Microsoft's sci-fi shooter *Halo* was supplanted in the public's affections by the superficially real-world *Call of Duty* juggernaut.

The Sega/Sammy conglomerate was determined to keep up the pace of releases on series that still turned a profit, but rushing *Sonic The Hedgehog [2006]* had severely damaged the brand. It was clear that the next core game in the franchise needed to be the result of a considerable rethink. Long-time Sonic fan Yoshihisa Hashimoto was placed in charge of development for the next instalment, which at this point bore the working title of *Sonic Adventure 3*. He was firmly instructed not to be constrained by a targeted release date.

With Hashimoto and his arm of Sonic Team vanishing into seclusion, 2007 and 2008 saw a conveyer belt of Sonic games from a variety of sources, in the hope that one might offer a compelling creative direction. The multi-media success of *Sonic X* was a distant memory, and Yuji Naka no longer offered a guiding hand to the hedgehog. A scattershot approach ensued.

Since 2001's hasty conversion of *Sonic Adventure 2* to Nintendo's Gamecube, there had been strong brand synergy between the Sonic franchise and the Kyoto hardware firm. Nintendo's primary audience remained Japanese schoolchildren, and this family market seemed well suited to Sonic's escapades.

The company's Wii console captured the public imagination to an unexpected degree. Building on the successful and innovative DS handheld, the hardware ostensibly did away with a conventional joypad. Games were instead played through a motion-sensitive rod superficially similar to a TV remote. Sega quickly agreed to support the new format, with Tetsu Katano taking the director's chair, supported by the members of Sonic Team not working under Hashimoto's instruction.

The project was originally referred to as *Sonic Wildfire*, with much development time devoted to simply finding a way of making the hedgehog work with motion-sensitive controls. It was regarded as a stopgap before *Sonic The Hedgehog [2006]* could be converted to the Wii from the more powerful Xbox 360 and Playstation 3. Given the poor reception of that title, however, Katano's project was given sole responsibility for establishing the Sonic on the new Nintendo system. Released in mid-2007 under the name *Sonic and the Secret Rings*, an Arabian Nights theme inspired the story and many of the settings.

The plot is constructed quite intelligently, with Sonic being sucked into a book one evening when dozing by the fire. (It's left ambiguous whether this is a literal description or whether he's just dropped off to sleep.) Inside the world of the book, he's drawn into a power struggle between two genies, being forced to locate the Secret Rings that control the book's reality. In a neat twist, because Sonic was the last person to read the book, many of its characters appear as he'd imagined them, based on his friends and enemies. For example, Knuckles takes the role of Sinbad. The Japanese developers do quite a good job of eking out a satisfactory number of semi-original level concepts from the middle-eastern scenario, with only brief excursions involving pirates and dinosaurs dispelling the mood somewhat.

Regrettably, the gameplay undoes all of this good work, with an utterly perverse implementation of the Wii controller sapping all entertainment from the title. While the game was initially described as playing like the sublime touchscreen sections of *Sonic Rush*, a wrong turn must have been taken somewhere in development. The finished title alternates between bland sprinting and over-complicated combat. The fact that jumping attacks must be charged-up means that the second half of the game is reliant on rote-learning of the levels.

Having to jolt the remote to perform a homing attack makes timing assaults unnecessarily difficult, and the unlockable selection of 'skill rings' mean that Sonic only intermittedly has access to his abilities. Despite being utterly terrible, the game sold reasonably well, and was soon being described as the first in a 'Sonic Storybook' sub-series, which would place the hedgehog in literature-inspired settings.

There's a striking piece of iconoclasm in *Sonic and the Secret Rings'* design, with the power-up structure that had been maintained since the first Mega Drive title being discarded in favour of pickups more suited to the gameplay. Most noticeably, the multi-ring items are simply a single ring with a number in front of it, instead of the usual smashable monitors. This move was overdue, with *Sonic The Hedgehog 2006's* adherence to the classic item boxes being clearly unnecessary. The invincibility pickup in particular was virtually useless, serving only as an opportunity to listen to the excellent riff from the game's main theme. In this respect, *Sonic and the Secret Rings* was a trendsetter, with the next core game abandoning all power-ups save for rings and extra lives.

Sonic Team USA were busy working with Iizuka's beloved NiGHTS character, but still found time to supervise another Western studio's experiments with the hedgehog. The result was *Sonic Rivals* for Sony's Playstation Portable handheld, with most of the work done by Canadian outfit Backbone Entertainment. The game modelled in polygons the classic 2D gameplay which the gaming media had been demanding for so long, but with a twist. The levels served as racetracks, with the player character only clearing the stage if he was able to beat an opponent to the goal.

In what marked an ongoing trend for the portable games, the title's plot saw an attack on Sonic's reality by Eggman Nega, with the scientist's parallel-universe counterpart apparently capable of the sort of nihilistic evil in which his conventional self was no longer allowed to indulge. *Sonic Rivals* met with little enthusiasm, and the race mechanic was regarded as an unnecessary complication, rather than a novel feature.

As might be expected, Sega's regular development partners also received commissions while Hashimoto and his colleagues were working on the next core title. *Sonic Rush Adventure* was produced by Dimps as a follow-up to its original DS title. In a change of approach, this game pitted Sonic against a group of pirates, with Eggman only entering the fray during the latter part of the game. At this point, it's revealed that Sonic & Tails have accidentally entered Blaze's dimension, with the mad scientist and his "Nega" counterpart having teamed up in a bid to destroy

Blaze's world. Despite some feeling that the level design had improved since the original *Sonic Rush*, that game's positive reception was not repeated, due to the need to repeatedly play through minigames in order to access the main action stages.

A second 'Rivals' game was also released on the Playstation Portable during 2007, from the original team at Backbone, with as lukewarm a response as the first effort. At this point, development of 2D Sonic games branched out into the new arena of mobile phones, with vertical platformer *Sonic Jump* being conceived to make maximum use of the devices' portrait screens.

Sega's growing links with Nintendo resulted in the announcement of a formal collaboration between the two companies, for a long-awaited Sonic and Mario crossover. The title came in a different form than expected, however, with the Wii and DS game consisting of minigames based on the Olympic Games. As holder of the rights to the sporting event, Sega developed the release, and publishing duties were shared between the two companies.

The firms felt that the use of their most iconic characters would increase the appeal of an Olympics title to children, and agreed that the formalised competition was a fitting banner under which to unite their mascots. Although *Mario and Sonic at the Olympic Games* had no plot as such, the choice of player characters drew extensively from both series' canons, with yet more figures making cameos as linesmen, judges, etc.

Released at the height of the Wii's mass-market dominance, the title embarrassingly sold better than recent Sonic games. A soft launch in late 2007 meant that the game was discounted to impulse-buy prices by the time that competition opened in Beijing six months later. There's not much artistic merit to discuss in the party game, beside the obvious aptness of the two nineties rivals long-awaited meeting being under the banner of the Olympic rings. The success of the venture lead to a series of follow-ups released at two-year intervals for each summer and winter competition. The other consequence was a drive to tie Sonic to Nintendo's extended family of Mario-related franchises, leading to the hedgehog appearing in the baffling-poplar *Super Smash Bros* fighting games.

The recruitment drive for developers even extended to Europe, and Sega turned to the UK, just as it had in the mid-nineties. Instead of Traveller's Tales, the group brought into the fold was Sumo Digital, a Sheffield-based codehouse which had built a reputation for quiet competence. They'd forged a relationship with Sega through converting the 2004 arcade title *Outrun 2* to several home systems, and were an obvious choice when the company sought a Sonic spin-off with sufficiently high production values to serve as a flagship release.

The result was *Sega Superstars Tennis*, taking part of its name from an Eyetoy camera minigame collection published a few years before. The game was favourably reviewed on release in spring 2008, with Sumo's faithful interpretation of several Sega franchises attracting considerable comment. Despite the absence of a narrative, several new voiceovers were recorded. This second-order release would have significant repercussions for the franchise in following years . . .

The final fruit of the outsourcing approach arrived in September 2008, in the form of *Sonic Chronicles: The Dark Brotherhood.* Fans had been advocating a Sonic role-playing game for several years, but the main appeal of the title lay in its development by genre-leaders Bioware, creators of *Baulder's Gate* and *Mass Effect.* Before release, comments from the developers sounded intriguing. Interviews suggested that the game would serve as a means of tying up loose plot threads from throughout the series, while repositioning Eggman as the primary antagonist. (His status having been undermined by his repeated duping by villains-of-the-month such as Chaos and Shadow.) The icing on the cake was the announcement that *Sonic R* composer Richard Jacques would return to the series in order to handle the music.

The reality of the game proved to be a massive disappointment, with lightweight RPG gameplay only the start of its problems. The art direction was extremely curious, with the look adopted neither replicating the traditional style of the Sonic titles nor showing sufficient inspiration justify the departure. It's all very well naming the first level "Green Hill Zone", but if it doesn't even slightly resemble the previous incarnations of that area, then there's very little point. The plot was also uninspired, with an initially-interesting story about a lost tribe of echidnas quickly discarded.

With hindsight, this may have been a blessing, as it was this element which attracted the attentions of former Archie writer Ken Penders. The writer had explored this subject in his comic scripts, and referred to the game in his writ against Sega. (See Chapter Four for details.) Back in the virtual world, Sonic and his friends soon found themselves warped to an alien planet, home to a hive-mind alien enemy clearly far more within Bioware's comfort zone.

Either the developer's heart was never in the title, or the firm's purchase by super-publisher Electronic Arts during creation of the game was a severe distraction. Development may also have been hampered by the lack of Sega oversight on the American continent. Once, Sonic Team USA would have been asked to undertake a watching brief, but the San Francisco outfit had been disbanded after completing work on the second NiGHTS game, with most staff returning to Japan.

The succession of games during 2007 and 2008 kept the series in the public's mind, but did little to remedy its reputation for substandard products, with only *Sega Superstars Tennis* meeting critics' expectations. The Olympics tie-in was alone in selling the numbers that the franchise would once have commanded. Behind closed doors, however, Sonic Team was working to a standard not seen since the Dreamcast years. The result of its labours would soon become apparent.

11. Unleashed and Boosted

Despite the blank cheque granted to Sonic Team to remedy the disappointing *Sonic The Hedgehog [2006]*, the revitalised developer needed just two years to complete its follow-up. Released in November 2008 under the name *Sonic Unleashed*, Yoshihisa Hashimoto's globe-trotting odyssey represented the apex of the storytelling style and techniques initiated by *Sonic Adventure*.

Key Game

Sonic Unleashed

Release : 2008

Origin : Japan

Global Sales : 1.83m

Metacritic Review Average : 57%

The plot repeated a trope familiar to the narrative-driven Sonic games, with Eggman attempting to utilise another elemental being. Despite having watched Sonic mopping up Chaos in *Sonic Adventure* and extinguishing Solaris in *Sonic The Hedgehog [2006]*, the scientist had no qualms about summoning Gaia, an earth-based monster. The opening of the game showed director Hashimoto's fan credentials clearly, with Eggman making a deliberate attempt to counter Sonic's deus ex machina 'Super' form. He then uses the resultant energy to awaken Gaia, splitting the Earth's crust into seven sections.

Sonic was accompanied by a slimmed-down cast of followers in his attempt to restore the shattered Earth using the Chaos Emeralds, and reverse the mutagenic effect of the Gaia creature on the planet's inhabitants. The simple story was plotted in detail, with an overall theme of balance and cycles. Sonic discovered that his amnesic new helper Chip was actually a being destined to defeat Gaia every time it awakened. In many ways the game provided a conclusion to the decade-long use of real-world locations as the inspiration for the latest 'Sonic Holiday', with the hedgehog touring many spots across the globe.

Foreign travel is the main theme behind the game, made explicit by Sonic's need to restore each continent, one at a time. After introductory sections of the title are concluded, an ally presents Sonic with a world map, from which he can select a location to visit as he hunts for the seven temples needed to re-empower the Chaos Emeralds. The main blessing that this theme gives the title takes the form the concepts for action stages. The real-world settings introduce variety into the designs and give boundless inspiration for set-pieces, saving the game from cliché. For example, the Hawaii stage isn't just a topical beach paradise, but features dense jungle, a couple of trips out to sea, collapsing ruins and a majestic waterfall. Though the initial Greek and Savannah stages don't match the sheer majesty of the levels to come, they still manage to establish memorable identities.

After the hedgehog recharges the Chaos Emeralds to restore the first two continents, the plot takes a back seat, with the game relying on Sonic's world tour and the people he meets on it to drive the story forward. Sonic is soon introduced to one-off character Professor Pickle, who happens hold the chair in "*big monsters that live in the Earth's core and need a slap*" at an Italian university. The Professor's guidance spearheads Sonic's efforts, and his rooms serve as a base where concept art, music and other unlocked bonuses can be accessed.

Pickle is the eponym of the game's affectionately stereotyped cast, being complemented by carefully-selected returning faces. Tails makes several appearances to provide Sonic with long-range transportation, and there are a number of cut-scenes featuring Amy. These are little more than cameos, however, and most of the time it's just Sonic and Chip who are exploring the globe.

Speaking of the deer-like flying sugar-seeker, Chip was by far and away the most satisfying gameplay hint mechanic included in the series to date. He had more than enough personality to make up for his distinctly odd design, and his addiction to all forms of dessert gave Sonic the idiot sidekick he'd been missing since *Sonic Adventure* reinvented Tails as a genius inventor to rival Eggman. The amnesic Chip's real identity was easy to predict for players of *Sonic The Hedgehog [2006]*, but the mystery didn't intrude on the action, being left in the background until the duo visit the penultimate Gaia temple.

The conversational cut-scene which follows this moment is striking, being far removed from what would be expected of the game. Like the *Sonic X* cartoon at its very peak, this exchange isn't high drama, but there's a trace of real emotion here, taking the title beyond the harmless fun usually associated with the series.

Looking at the opposition, Eggman was supplied with the latest in a long-running series of robot minions in the form of androids Orbot and Cubot. These bumbling mechanoids proved to have an unusual degree of staying power, being featured in subsequent Sonic games for over five years.

The effort expended on the adventure's themes and narrative was matched by a complete gameplay reinvention. Since 1998, the two central elements of Sonic's 3D outings were his homing spin attack, which allowed his signature move to function without any tricky judgement of depth, and the light speed dash which briefly confined Sonic to trails of rings as he was transported around the level. Although these moves were retained by Sonic Team, they were adjusted to create a very different experience.

The aim wasn't to translate the play mechanics from the 16-bit games into 3D, but to find a way of allowing the player to achieve the stunts and freedom of movement seen in Sonic's cartoon adventures. The result appealed strongly to long-time fans, who could finally achieve during gameplay the sort of showboating and tricks showcased by the much-loved introduction to *Sonic The Hedgehog CD*. Bizarrely, the key to this transformation was a less-than successful gameplay element first introduced by Dimps.

In *Sonic Rush* on the Nintendo DS, the 'Boost' button betrayed a fundamental misunderstanding of the how Sonic should work in a 2D environment. Powered by a ring-charged meter, the Boost function allowed Sonic to instantly accelerate forward at full speed, his velocity maintained for as long as his stored energy would allow. This turned the game's zones into bland race tracks, with none of the depth of design found during the 16-bit 2D titles.

Hashimoto, on the other hand, saw the potential for a 3D game in the concept. With the camera poisoned behind Sonic, allowing the player to see ahead, the Boost is a different proposition. The pseudo real-world setting makes sprinting through the flat-out sections of the action stages irresistible, with the cartoon hedgehog practically laughing at the more ordinary world he powers through. The moment where the high-concept behind the revised gameplay is revealed to the player is in the Rome level, as Sonic accelerates to keep up with jet-propelled flying badniks along the course of a ruined aqueduct. When the Boost is fully deployed, standard enemies, let alone the architecture, become static irrelevances. The player's focus is solely on the hedgehog and the lighting-quick enemies he pursues.

Boosting finally brought the sheer pace of the Mega Drive titles into the 3D series, but Sonic Team made another, vital addition. The missing link in the character's arsenal was finally granted by allowing him to Boost in mid-air, encouraging continual forward motion at all times. These changes to Sonic's handling broadened his freedom of movement to match player's instinctive judgement of what the hedgehog should be capable of.

The backbone of the game's achievements was Sega's new proprietary multi-format graphics engine, dubbed 'Hedgehog'. The emergence of this technology was undeniably late, with rival publisher Capcom first deploying its competing Framework system over two years before. The engine had a particular affinity at organic texturing, giving a distinctive atmosphere to each level not found in any prior game. From the whitewashed walls of the Greek opening stage to mist-covered Chinese foothills, each area feels not only unique but alive.

The engine's only stumble comes during one of the later stages. Faced with Sonic sprinting full-pelt through a Hawaiian jungle, with a level of detail not expected until the next generation of consoles, the engine visibly buckles, with slowdown and animation frames skipped. The moments when the same level works more than compensate for these errors, though, and it's hard to escape the feeling that Sonic Team deliberately set out to break the technology, just to establish its limitations.

Tomoya Ohtani once again led the sound team, supported by Sonic Team veterans Fumie Kumatani and Kenichi Tokoi. The latter's superb score for the otherwise diabolically-poor *Sonic and the Secret Rings* proved him more than deserving of a return to the main titles. The soundtrack isn't the series' strongest, with a main rock theme in the Senoue vein a distinctly forced inclusion, and Ohtani makes less effort than his colleagues to reflect the host nations' influences in his action stage music.

Negative feedback on the large cast of characters in the 2006 title had been taken on-board, and Sonic was the only controllable hero. Sonic Team still wished to supply more than one playstyle, however, and so the plot had the hedgehog falling under Gaia's influence at night. The resultant transformation into a snarling beast unlocked a series of simplistic beat-em-up stages to complement the usual high-speed action.

In the West, the game's marketing campaign centred on his transformation into a 'werehog', and the release's name was changed to emphasise this. (As most reviewers pointed out, Sonic's night-time form was technically a Hedgewolf, but the Japanese-speaking developers were not particularly concerned by the niceties of Latin.) A five-minute CGI animation was commissioned, entitled *Night of the Werehog*, to ram the message home. Sega of Japan preferred to market the game on its globe-trotting aspects, with the release's Asian title being *Sonic World Adventure*.

The werehog stages changed noticeably over the course of the game, with the uncomplicated fighting areas initially offered replaced with precision platforming in New York and Iran. The main problem was that these levels seem to be presented in the wrong order, with Sonic faced with an array of platforming challenges only after he's unlocked enough moves for fighting to actually be enjoyable. Beating enemies allows Sonic to collect yellow crystals needed to improve the Werehog's various attributes, but it's not made clear just how many moves can be unlocked by sinking experience points into the 'Combat' stat. The gameplay experience on Xbox 360 and Playstation 3 was largely identical, but a cut-down version of the title was released for the Wii and Playstation 2, developed by Dimps.

For most critics, and a significant portion of the public, the deficiencies of the werehog sections overshadowed the rest of the game, leading to review scores not much higher than *Sonic The Hedgehog [2006]*. Sega was rightly not discouraged by this, and the next two main titles would reproduce the *Sonic Unleashed* daytime stage gameplay wholesale, to an extremely positive reception.

Fans certainly appreciated the enormous leap in quality that the series had taken, although their joy was tempered by Hashimoto's departure from Sega after completing *Sonic Unleashed*. Having finished work on the project, he moved to role-playing-game specialists Square Enix, where he continues to hold a senior role. He bequeathed to his successors a Sonic who had once again found his feet, but would miss the strength of vision which had momentarily been brought to bear.

The misfortune of Hashimoto's resignation was compounded in early 2009 by the release of *Sonic and the Black Knight*, a staggeringly poor second entry in the 'Sonic Storybook' sub-series. Tetsu Katano intended for this strand to continue as a group of Wii-exclusive titles, and the hedgehog this time found himself sucked into Arthurian legends. Key roles were taken by familiar faces, as in *Sonic and the Secret Rings*. Superb presentation could not mask a further deterioration of gameplay, however, and the release attracted the poorest reviews of any full-budget Sonic title.

Plans for any further Sonic Storybook titles were abruptly cancelled, and it became clear that Sonic Team's 2006 fall from grace and Katano's replacement of Yuji Naka were linked. Takashi Iizuka was promptly appointed to a general producer role on the Sonic series, with the former head of Sonic Team USA now charged with providing a consistent creative direction for the hedgehog.

12. Mr Iizuka Takes Charge

Takashi Iizuka inherited a strong gameplay template for future titles from *Sonic Unleashed*, and his first order of business on taking direct control of the Sonic series was to supply a consistent narrative tone to complement this sold base.

With development launched on two separate platform games, he commissioned carefully-targeted spin-offs from studios outside of Sega to maintain a steady flow of titles, while avoiding rushed disappointments such as *Sonic The Hedgehog [2006]*. Generally speaking, developers who had performed well with the series previously were deployed more strategically, working on titles more conceptually-aligned to the core output of Sonic Team.

The success of Sumo Digital's 2008 tennis game resulted in the firm being commissioned to produce a bigger-budgeted title, with a more broadly-appealing racing theme. As might be deduced from the name, *Sonic & Sega All-Stars Racing* put the hedgehog and his franchise firmly centre-stage, with several less-successful Sega ventures dropped to make room in the cast and track rosters. While some corners were obviously cut in development, the result was sufficiently accomplished for the videogame press to now treat the All-Stars series as a sub-division of the Sonic brand, instead of a Sega fan curio.

Part of the game's success was due to Sumo's persistence in prototyping. The developer was willing to stand firm in the face of wry comment on the hedgehog's driving a car, and the obvious question of why a character famed for his speed could not win the races on foot. Sumo's public statement that Sonic's love of competition led him to handicap himself by driving was a charming moment of fan-engagement from the company. In reality, gameplay tests had shown that a small vehicle-less character unbalanced the aggressive racing gameplay when pitted against larger car-driving opponents.

The title was released for a large number of systems, and played a part in Sega's push into mobile gaming, with cut-down iOS and Android releases ensuing. Sumo did not attempt to add any plot or story mode to the crossover title. The most instructive aspect of its depiction of Sonic is in confirming the dominance of the *Sonic Heroes* aesthetic; all but one of the Sonic-inspired tracks are themed around levels from that game.

The cost-saving measures included keeping original music to a minimum, with Richard Jacques compiling a soundtrack from existing recordings. The exception was a striking theme song from English singer/songwriter Bentley Jones. The musician, a long-time Sonic fan, had collaborated with Jun Senoue on the score for *Shadow The Hedgehog*, before launching a successful music career of his own in Japan. Sadly *Sonic & Sega All-Stars Racing* was some of the last work that Jones carried out on the series. The artist parted ways with Sega after attacking the company for using some of his remixes without asking his permission.

The sales and critical acclaim achieved by *Sonic & Sega All-Stars Racing* dwarfed 2010's other spin-off release. This was a final hangover from the production-line of insipid low-profile titles during the first half of the seventh console generation, being a final release in the Sonic Riders series. Exclusive to Microsoft's Kinnect hardware, it's difficult to believe that *Sonic Free Riders* did not owe its existence solely to an incentive payment from the manufacturer to put the hedgehog on its universally-derided Xbox 360 add-on.

Over the course of 2010, the shift in the series' direction under Iizuka's stewardship became clear. The sprawling casts of the previous decade's Sonic titles were curtailed, in favour of a tight focus on the characters introduced during the Mega Drive years. More surprising was the producer's dismissal of the Earth-like settings which he himself had used as a director in *Sonic Adventure 2* and *Shadow The Hedgehog*. The military force of GUN was absent from the games, as were human beings in general, save for Eggman.

It's possible that Iizuka felt that *Sonic Unleashed* naturally marked the peak of the real-world settings, and that a change would be better the reusing them with diminishing returns. Alternatively, his thinking may have stemmed from a desire to return to the fantasy settings of the Mega Drive years. This idea was supported by the renewed presence of animal-shaped badniks as Eggman's foot soldiers, in place of the more generic robots which the scientist had taken to deploying.

It's most likely that the new approach was simply about reducing risk; if *Sonic and Sega All-Stars Racing* could be popular with both reviewers and the public despite having no plot, then downplaying story elements in the main Sonic games appeared the least-perilous approach, given the drubbing handed out to the plot-heavy *Sonic The Hedgehog [2006]*.

The new ethos chimed with some expectations of the series, appealing to long-time fans while presenting an easy-to-grasp concept for children approaching the franchise for the first time. The price was alienating those whose first experience of Sonic had been as the sociable star of epic adventures. The relative lack of impact that the Mega Drive games had produced in Japan compared to the west created some other issues. In particular, the new iteration of Sonic Team did not appear to place as much value on certain iconic elements as western fans.

Sonic The Hedgehog 4 is the best case study for the awkwardness which Sega showed in the years leading up to the character's 20th birthday. The game was a standard 2D Sonic platformer, released for the digital marketplaces of home consoles, as well as mobile phones, but the marketing and promotion of the title is arguably more interesting than the content it provided.

The game was the subject of an extremely well-judged publicity campaign, with the first reveal trailer being a remarkably astute piece of work. The game was initially codenamed 'Project Needlemouse', the working title for the original Mega Drive release, in a bid to portray it as a return to the roots of the series. When the final title was confirmed, it suggested an intention to reintroduce the character as perfectly suited to the new downloadable-game market. This raised hopes of a 2D game to stand shoulder-to-shoulder with the 16-bit classics, as opposed to the middle-of-the-road efforts by Dimps.

The difficulty is that the final product is nothing of the sort; it's simply that exact same Dimps team working for home systems instead of Nintendo's portable machines. The physics model shares many of the flaws and glitches of its handheld predecessors, such the ability to persuade Sonic to stand on ceilings. This was a longstanding bugbear with Dimps' work, arising from the programming tricks they used to mimic the Mega Drive games' physics. A longstanding rumour maintains that Yuji Naka denied permission for Dimps to be handed the source code to his original works, but this is difficult to credit. Dimps' projects have always been released with the Sonic Team branding, and Naka personally oversaw its first four titles.

The leaden handling of Sonic in the game was another marked contrast to the 16-bit classics whose approach *Sonic The Hedgehog 4* was supposed to directly continue. Gamers were given an unintended preview of the title when it was uploaded to Microsoft's Partnernet service, used to distribute work-in-progress content between licensed developers. For most downloadable games, this provided useful feedback, but for such a high-profile release, it resulted in the incomplete title being picked apart by a ferociously dedicated audience.

The defective physics were the subject of particular criticism, and inconsistencies with the original games, such as the loss of the traditional 'spinning legs' running animation, attracted further complaints. The build exposed the game's iPhone origins, with several acts of the leaked Xbox 360 release featuring botched implementations of concepts obviously designed for gyroscopic or touchscreen input. In the face of the outcry, Sega postponed the title by several months in an attempt to mitigate its shortcomings.

It's an acceptable platform game on its own terms, but begged the question of why label the title *Sonic The Hedgehog 4* if the intention was simply to continue with the modern-day 2D portrayal of the character? Amongst casual fans, the use of the standard green-eyed Sonic design came as a surprise to those who expected a return of the less streamlined original model of the character. The only real link between the promotional campaign and the finished product is a depressing one; the recycling of level themes, with environments and bosses heavily inspired by fondly-remembered areas from the first two games.

Jun Senoue, at least, seemed to get the message, but his drum-sample heavy soundtrack isn't entirely successful as a Masato Nakamura pastiche, aside from a boss theme originally intended for 1995's *Sonic 3D*. Senoue's involvement as composer is arguably the only thing elevating the title above most of Dimps' output. The game attracted positive reviews, but word-of-mouth was poor, and the proposed *Episode Two* follow-up was not the subject of particular anticipation.

When announcing *Sonic The Hedgehog 4*, Sega had claimed that it would follow the bite-sized gaming concept pioneered by Valve in its *Half Life* Episodes; smaller instalments of titles released at regular intervals. Like Valve, however, it would find it rather difficult to turn this concept into reality, and two years would pass before the *Sonic The Hedgehog 4* sub-series reared its head again.

The debacle appeared to prompt some soul-searching inside Sega, particularly in the west. The promotional campaign for the title had been extremely successful, obtaining a level of media and public attention disproportionate to a downloadable game. In the end, it was let down by the actual content delivered by Sega of Japan. Since 1997, all of the decisions surrounding Sonic had come from the east, with only Archie's comic series deviating from the parent company's line. But sales of the Sonic titles had been falling steadily for several years, and the Sega subsidiaries of 2010 were not the same as those of a decade before.

Sega Europe had achieved considerable success under Chief Operating Officer Mike Hayes in its stewardship of the Football Manager and Total War strategy titles. The company had effectively taken control of the US branch in 2009, with Hayes leading both organisations. Unsurprisingly, the large and active online Sonic fanbase had begun to migrate into the company, with community managers such as Kevin Eva and Aaron Webber being strongly rooted in the movement. While Iizuka's Sonic Team retained the final say in any decision related to the character, the western divisions of Sega became more active in their efforts to sell Sonic, and in advising their Japanese colleagues on their perception of the market's desires.

A key step was the recruitment of a brand director for the Sonic series. Former Sega Europe marketing manager David Corless took on the daunting task of co-ordinating the large array of small merchandise licences which still remained let, and ensuring that the revised conception of Sonic coming from Iizuka was reflected globally. Most of this work occurred behind the schemes, but a public sign of Corless's housekeeping occurred in the second half of 2010, when several Sonic games disappeared from sale through digital marketplaces.

The brand manager confirmed that the deletion was initiated by Sega, which had decided to remove from sale titles which failed to meet an undisclosed score on the review aggregate website Metacritic.com. Tacit admissions of poor product quality from Sega had so far been rare, but the western divisions were obviously gaining confidence in dealing with the Japanese hub. The impact of Metacritic.com on the games industry has not been wholly beneficial, with its herd mentality and focus on review scores leaving little room for more nuanced artistic judgements. In this instance, though, its facilitation of quality vetting was undeniably welcome.

The culmination of this drive would eventually surface in 2014, but some signs were immediately apparent, such as recasting the western voice artists working on the series. The performers introduced with the western localisation of the *Sonic X* cartoon were dismissed, with the noticeable exception of Mike Pollock, whose performance as Eggman had become synonymous with the character.

A new team was introduced, lead by Roger Craig Smith as Sonic. The fanbase had still not entirely warmed to the departing Jason Griffith, and welcomed Smith with open arms. The actor seemed happy to reciprocate; the author was one of a number of Sonic fans who met him during a publicity appearance in late 2010, and he was charm itself, being more than happy to discuss his work in the role.

Roger Craig Smith's first significant performance as the hedgehog was for *Sonic Colours*, one of two core Sonic games put into development at Sonic Team on completion of Unleashed. The title was released for the Nintendo Wii in the run-up to Christmas 2010. It had drawn development talent from a variety of sources, including members of the Unleashed group and the disbanded Storybook outfit. For the first time since the Adventure games, we see a direct continuation of gameplay from the previous instalment, with the action handling exactly like the daytime stages of *Sonic Unleashed.*

In terms of tone and storytelling, however, there is a marked shift, with Iizuka's new approach making itself felt. There's a distinct simplification of content. Instead of the large cast and grandiose story of *Sonic Unleashed*, we have a much smaller-scale, Looney Toons feel to the plot, which sees Eggman opening an orbital amusement park, as a cover for his plan to enslave an alien race. It's tempting to cite the arrival of regular series writers Warren Graff and Ken Pontac as the reason for the shift in mood, but given the centralised control of the franchise, the scribes would simply work with plots prescribed to them by Sega Japan.

The game is reduced to a cast of six; Sonic and Tails take centre-stage, although the latter is present only in cut-scenes, assisted by a representative of the alien species. Eggman provides the opposition, together with Orbot & Cubot acting as a combination of light relief and a reason to force the scientist to explain his scheme. In a move obviously inspired by the successful Wii *Super Mario Galaxy* titles, each of the environments is labelled a planet. The theme park setting is used as a pretext for fantasy-themed environments, such as a world of sweets and a vast Asian aquarium.

Two gameplay expansions are introduced to the Unleashed model; a new line of power-ups granted by merging with the alien 'wisps', and underwater levels. The latter are a real triumph, being the first time that this key gameplay mechanic from the Mega Drive titles had been successfully deployed in the modern era, and put the Adventure games' aquatic dabblings to shame.

Key Game

Sonic Colours

Release : 2010

Origin : Japan

Global Sales : 1.58m

Metacritic Review Average : 78%

The choice of the Wii as development platform was understandable; there was a strong cross-over in audience between Nintendo's all-ages system and the cartoon hedgehog. The standard-definition technical set-up of the machine also allowed development costs to be kept low. The compromises are clear, however. The overworld of *Sonic Unleashed* is replaced by a series of map screens, and environments which would take the form of one continuous ten-minute level on the Xbox 360 or Playstation 3 are broken down into up to eight acts, hampering the coherency of the world. To make matters worse, the grainy standard-definition visuals of *Sonic Colours* are difficult to return to after the gorgeous environments of *Sonic Unleashed*.

Tomoya Ohtani retained the post of music director, following his work on *Sonic The Hedgehog [2006]* and *Sonic Unleashed*. His soundtrack was unfortunately less effective than for those games. At the time, it was easy to suspect that the composer was simply jaded on his third consecutive Sonic game. His work was reminiscent of Jun Senoue's score for *Shadow The Hedgehog*. In both cases, occasional flashes of the talent which secured the musician's place in the franchise's history only add to the impression that the volume of music required means that Sonic games are best tackled by a rotating bank of composers.

Ohtani's subsequent work has shown that this was not the case, however, with a consciously adopted new musical style of less forceful compositions and softer electronic work. The composer provided a strong main theme song for the game, which also served as the background music for the first set of levels, but the vocal version by members of American pop outfit Cash Cash felt like a forced inclusion.

For the first time since *Sonic The Hedgehog 2*, a major home console title was converted to handheld systems, allowing for a dual launch. Dimps were tasked with creating a Nintendo DS version of the title, as a 2D platformer in the mould of *Sonic Rush*.

Sonic Colours was a successful game, with the exorcising of *Sonic Unleashed*'s werehog leading to higher review scores, and over 1.5m copes were sold. There were a number of weaknesses in the title, however, that left those who appreciated its predecessor's strengths slightly underwhelmed. The level designs are not as distinctive as those of *Sonic Unleashed*, and the shift in narrative tone leaves the adventure feeling more throwaway.

Aside from the remarkable wildflower-meadows of the Planet Wisp area, the levels feel like generic backdrops pasted onto a gameplay mechanic designed in isolation, instead of convincing as places. Graff and Pontac's work as writers is curious. There's definitely a more authored tone to the characters' dialogue, and you feel that professionals are at work, but the cut-scenes feel more like stand-alone sketches than tools to drive the story forward.

The game capped a reasonably stable year for the franchise, and Iizuka's approach was now bedded in. But the producer found himself facing a new challenge for 2011; balancing his preference for uncomplicated stand-alone adventures against the demands of adequately celebrating Sonic's 20th birthday.

13. The Birthday Party

Sega had made an effort to acknowledge 10 years of Sonic, with an anniversary logo plastered across *Sonic Adventure 2*, but that title would clearly have been released regardless of the occasion. In 2011, the hedgehog's 20th birthday celebrations were a very different affair, anchored by big-budget nostalgia title *Sonic Generations*. While *Sonic Colours* had been very much orientated towards children, and attempted to win new fans, 2011's release was seen as an opportunity to appeal to an older audience, and so development was launched on the Xbox 360 and Playstation 3, rather than the Wii.

After the issues encountered over *Sonic The Hedgehog 4*'s promotional strategy, a more co-ordinated approach was taken, with the final product being extremely close to that suggested by the media campaign. The expected *Episode Two* instalment of the downloadable title was put on hold, ostensibly to allow for an uninterrupted media focus on *Sonic Generations*, although the need to release Dimps staff to create a handheld version of that game probably played a part.

The 20th anniversary was the point at which Britain's Summer Of Sonic convention came of age. The brainchild of fansite owner Svend Joscelyne, the one-day event had been held annually since 2008, growing in stature each year. Despite its ongoing success, and visible support from Sega Europe orchestrated by Kevin Eva, it remained strictly fan-led, with a large committee sharing organising duties.

The success of Summer of Sonic created several issues, with the convention perpetually relocating to a different South-of-England venue each year in a bid to increase its capacity. The constantly growing popularity of the event is a testament to the fondness with which the UK views Sonic, and also served to highlight the catalytic role of *Sonic The Comic* in creating the UK fanbase.

Initially, the array of guests was drawn solely from UK creators behind the franchise. The writers and artists of *Sonic The Comic* became regular attendees, being pleased, if slightly baffled, at the affection in which their work was held. Live performances of music from the games have become a key selling point of Summer of Sonic meetings, and Jun Senoue has been one of the most enthusiastic overseas guests, attending the majority of the gatherings. Although since dwarfed by subsequent conventions, at the time the 2011 meeting was the easily the largest to have been organised.

The guests of honour were Sonic Team chief Takashi Iizuka and Yuji Naka. Although Naka had publically left Sega in 2006, the firm remained a key investor in his development house Prope, and he was happy to undertake publicity work for the Sonic series. The former programmer conducted a question & answer session from the main stage and signed copies of games.

The success of Summer of Sonic lead Sega's US arm to introduce its own annual event, Sonic Boom, although this was a more corporate-driven and controlled venture than its endearingly spontaneous inspiration. Summer of Sonic's Achilles heel has always been capacity. The organisers are commendably committed to keeping the event free to attend, but pre-registration is mandatory to control numbers. In 2011, all tickets were claimed within three minutes of being made available; the 2013 convention was 'sold out' within nine seconds.

Turning to the anniversary game itself, *Sonic Generations* contained remakes of levels drawn from the character's twenty year history, each presented as two acts. The first of these was played by 'Classic Sonic', the chubby pale-blue character who appeared in the 1991 Mega Drive title. Although modelled in 3D, his gameplay stuck to a 2D axis, doing a better job of replicating the original gamestyle than Dimps had managed in over a decade of attempts.

Alongside this, the taller, deep blue, green-eyed 'Modern Sonic' tackled each stage in the now-familiar *Sonic Unleashed* style. He swapped between 3D and 2D control mechanisms as the levels alternated between fast-paced action sections and more precise platforming. Sonic Team had clearly learnt much from the *Sonic The Hedgehog 4* outcry, and Classic Sonic was pointedly denied use of his modern counterpart's homing attack. The anachronistic inclusion of this gameplay trait had recently attracted much abuse to the downloadable title.

The choice of games to be represented in *Sonic Generations* was relatively uncontroversial, with one area drawn from each high-profile release. The only aspect that raised an eyebrow was the decision to regard *Sonic The Hedgehog 3* and *Sonic & Knuckles* as one title, being represented only by a recreation of the latter's Sky Sanctuary Zone. Sonic Team were informed in its level selection by an internet poll, but didn't regard the result as binding. Presenting a balanced array of concepts and play styles took precedence over meeting every fan expectation.

In general, the game is remarkably well-judged, with Jun Senoue and his colleagues' approach to the music being a case in point. In each level, the incarnation of Sonic which originally tackled that stage is accompanied by a straight re-recoding of the original background music, while their counterpart runs to a re-arrangement of that same tune.

> ## Key Game
>
> ### *Sonic Generations*
>
> **Release :** 2011
>
> **Origin :** Japan
>
> **Global Sales :** 2.43m
>
> **Metacritic Review Average :** 77%

Masato Nakamura retained all rights to his tracks from *Sonic The Hedgehog* and its sequel, normally rendering them off-limits for inclusion in new Sonic games. The anniversary, however, was a sufficient occasion for Sega to pay the licensing fees required. Senoue's joy in finally getting to play with the compositions which had inspired his work is audible, but the highlight of the soundtrack is Cash Cash's relentless reinterpretation of the Big Arms boss theme from *Sonic The Hedgehog 3*. The band's Alex Makhlouf is a long-time Sonic fan, and the cause of their involvement with the series.

For the most part, the levels in *Sonic Generations* do justice to their original incarnations, although there's some weak design in the update of *Sonic Colours*' Planet Wisp. In each case, Sonic Team manage to expand the original level concept slightly; the Chemical Plant Zone from *Sonic The Hedgehog 2* gains some aerial action sequences as Modern Sonic swings from cranes high above the factory, while *Sonic Adventure*'s Speed Highway is enlivened by sequences where Sonic ploughs through the high-rise buildings that he once simply sprinted past. Credit has to be given to Sonic Team for its willingness to face past mistakes. After the nightmare *of Sonic The Hedgehog [2006]*, the temptation to ignore the title must have been strong, but that game's Crisis City is included in a polished form that lays to rest its original buggy and fractured incarnation.

In keeping with the narrative tone of *Sonic Colours*, the story is perfunctory, with writers Warren Graff & Ken Pontac keeping the focus squarely on Sonic and Tails in the short cut-scenes which bookend the action. The plot is the bare minimum needed to dignify the game's concept, with both Sonics dragged out of their native time zones and investigating the presence of isolated chunks of the past within a mysterious white space.

Sonic Generations' sole narrative departure from the predictable lies in the structure of the plot, presumably devised by Sonic Team. Since 1998's *Sonic Adventure*, a tradition had emerged of Eggman's new weapon (Perfect Chaos, Shadow, Neo Metal Sonic) escaping his control and wrecking havoc. Here, that trope is reversed, with the scientist being revealed as being in control of the monstrous Time Eater entity, despite initially posing as being at its mercy.

A couple of years later, Pontac revealed that he had little background knowledge of Sonic's history. Once he and Graff had accepted the unofficial title of series writers, he had based his work on reading online character summaries and viewing a number of past cutscenes on YouTube. It's hard not to view some continuity problems in *Sonic Generations* in the light of this, and the Sonic community predictably erupted in outrage.

No fanbase is loveable while frothing at the mouth, and there was a distinct lack of proportion to the views aired, but Pontac's position is difficult to endorse. The simplified approach which and Graff had taken stood as a noticeable contrast to the previous decade's worth of storytelling. It was made harder to accept by the knowledge that it was devised in ignorance of what had gone before, rather than as a deliberate shift of approach.

Admittedly, it's slightly unfair to single out the writers, as their ethos will obviously have met with the approval of Iizuka and his fellow Sonic Team senior managers. The slimmed-down storytelling is in the vein of Disney short cartoons, rather than the anime reachings of the Adventure games and *Sonic Unleashed*.

The handheld port of the title saw Dimps becoming slightly more ambitious as a result of its move to the new Nintendo 3DS, fully modelling the game in 3D, instead of the customary sprites. The portable incarnation attracted more attention than *Sonic Colours'* handheld release due to the inclusion of different levels from the home console title, representing the same games through different examples. Unfortunately, Dimps was constrained by its decision not to attempt 3D gameplay in Modern Sonic's acts, leaving the two hedgehogs playstyles' virtually indistinguishable, and removing much of the appeal.

Sega's customer engagement for *Sonic Generations* was exemplary. There was sufficient confidence in the product to release a one-act demo in June 2011 to celebrate the actual anniversary of *Sonic The Hedgehog*'s release, several months in advance of the November retail launch of *Sonic Generations*. Now having a greater understanding of the dedicated grown-up fanbase following the franchise, the company unveiled a lavish £100 collector's edition of the title. This included a soundtrack CD, a book, a statue and all the paraphernalia more associated with more high-profile western releases such as *Assassins' Creed* and *Call of Duty*.

While the UK's Game chain declined to stock the item, believing there to be no demand, Sega's market research was atypically accurate, and the collection quickly sold out in other retailers. In general, *Sonic Generations* was a triumph, continuing the general goodwill which *Sonic Colours* had obtained from the gaming media.

The release of the anniversary title marked the end of a long term project commenced on completion of *Sonic Unleashed*. Sonic Team took its now-customary step back from the limelight, relying on trusted collaborators to keep the hedgehog in the public mind. The next title to be released was the long-delayed second instalment of *Sonic The Hedgehog 4*, a full two years after first part of this supposedly episodic adventure. The reason for the time elapsed was immediately apparent, with *Episode One*'s sprites having been replaced by fully 3D modelling, and gameplay mechanics completely altered by the inclusion of Tails.

Many of the gameplay tricks which required a second joypad in Sonic *The Hedgehog 3* were repurposed to work through one controller only, and a faintly-dubious move was introduced where Sonic and his sidekick snuggle up to form a combined spin attack to destroy larger enemies.

As usual when Sega is keen to obtain fan goodwill, Metal Sonic was dragged into the action as a recurring boss. The android was the playable lead character in the bonus chapter *Episode Metal* made available to *Episode Two* players who'd also purchased the first instalment.

This additional download saw the robot tackling an edited highlights package of levels from the first part of the game. The sprite-based graphics approach from that outing was retained, but the physics closely resembled the improved iteration in *Episode Two*, somewhat undermining the protestations from Sega that it would have been impossible to improve *Episode One*'s flaws through downloadable patches.

Initially, *Sonic The Hedgehog 4: Episode Two* appears to be as insipid as its predecessor, notwithstanding the improvements in the physics model. At the halfway-point in the game, however, something rather wonderful happens. From the Oil Desert Zone onwards, there's a considerable leap in the quality of level design, and the final stages of the game are genuinely excellent, cunningly deploying the advantages of 3D modelling to update and revitalise 16-bit gameplay elements.

Sega obviously had high hopes for the title, and spokespeople professed themselves baffled at the middling review scores it attracted, commenting that they felt it to be a better game than the better-rated *Episode One*. They were right, of course, but since the first instalment's release, *Sonic Generations'* Classic Sonic levels had reminded the critics of the authentic playstyle of 2D Sonic, raising the bar in the minds of both reviewers and the general public. In the face of this muted reception, plans for a third instalment appear to have been quietly dropped.

The middle-ground approach of *Sonic The Hedgehog 4* was abandoned, and it seemed decided that Iizuka's Sonic would only appear in Sonic Team-controlled big-budget Christmas-released extravaganzas, and minor titles for the exponentially-expanding iOS and Android markets.

But Sega's western divisions had other ideas...

Into The Future

(2013 – Present)

14. Several Wills

With the 20th anniversary successfully negotiated, the Sonic franchise appeared to be in an uncharacteristically stable condition. Takashi Iizuka's approach to the character was well-understood, if not universally loved, and a solid array of development teams appeared able to release high-quality Sonic games at regular intervals, across several genres. The *Sonic Unleashed* gameplay systems were fully bedded in as standard for the series, combining the high-speed spectacle of the Adventure days with the retro appeal and precision platforming of the 2D approach.

While the intricate plots of earlier titles had vanished, Warren Graff and Ken Pontac's jokes were on the money, and their writing was a dependable and consistent element. Sega's November slot in the annual video game release calendar was secure, and it was able to exert sufficient control over its development teams to ensure games were available to fill it. Merchandise was selling well, with a comprehensive range of licences for the modern design of the character being quietly complemented, in the UK at least, by an old-school range featuring the original incarnation.

Behind the scenes, however, an amicable split between the eastern and western Sega divisions was emerging. The second half of the seventh console generation had polarised the differences in the global marketplaces. The popularity of home consoles had fallen considerably in Japan, in favour of mobile gaming. The west, however, remained wedded to blockbuster releases, despite other shifts in taste. These differences were reflected in rival aspirations for Sonic.

Something had to give.

The smartphone gaming market on both sides of the Pacific was too lucrative to be ignored, even if the missteps around *Sonic The Hedgehog 4* had stymied Sega's first attempt to properly establish a foothold. For the second serious offensive, the company decided to engage a specialist developer, rather than continue to employ longstanding handheld veterans Dimps.

The team used was Hardlight, a Sega subsidiary formed in the UK during 2012, using staff released by closure of the Sega Racing Studio. The developer's first project was an iOS/Android update of the several-years-old *Sonic Jump*, to slot into the sub-genre of Doodle Jump clones. The result was a competent gyroscope input mini-game which enjoyed reasonable success, but several factors held it back. The level-based structure was noticeably inappropriate for seamless mobile play, and spikes in the difficulty level dogged the game.

The same team struck gold a year later, however, with its follow-up *Sonic Dash*. This brazenly appropriated the gameplay from popular app Temple Run, but well-judged controls and beautiful art direction allowed it to weather allegations of plagiarism. The setting was an attractive update of *Sonic Heroes'* Seaside Hill, with a new nautically-themed area added to give more variety to the backdrops. Unlike *Sonic Jump*, *Sonic Dash* was free to play, and attracted strong criticism from some for its inclusion of microtransactions.

On balance, though, this anger seems misplaced. While the inclusion of pay-to-win mechanics in sold games is to be condemned, it seems an acceptable element in titles such as Dash, and the game was reasonably generous. There was plenty of fun to be had without paying a penny, so long as players resigned themselves to sticking with Sonic as their sole payable character. It was only the cosmetic change of unlocking the likes of Knuckles which really forced the player to part with money; the core gameplay was available to all. Hardlight steadily added content, with more characters introduced by online-focussed global score targets, and set-pieces introduced to promote other titles in the series.

With *Sonic Colours* and *Sonic Generations*, Sega had quietly annualised the franchise, with a release in November maximising pre-Christmas revenue, and the Sonic games' traditional long tail of discounted sales carrying through until the market's summer shutdown. To keep to momentum going, the next in Sumo's All-Stars titles was moved into the November slot, being Sega's big release for late 2012. *Sonic & All-Stars Racing Transformed* was a direct sequel to the previous effort from

Sheffield's finest. The spotlight focus remained on Sonic for the mass-market, with copious fan-service of forgotten Sega franchises like Panzer Dragoon and NiGHTS to ensure blanket adoption by the company's long-time customers.

The budget limitations which had dogged the 2010 release were long gone, with sumptuous visuals and remixed music overseen by Richard Jacques. A genuinely modern video game, All-Stars seemed to appeal to all sectors of its audience, and its success was sufficient to prompt speculation on a crossover with the long-established Mario Kart series.

Sonic & All-Stars Racing Transformed was the last release to be published under the regime established in 2009. The dissolution of Sonic's global identity occurred over the course of a year, from early 2013, when Sega of Japan announced that for at least the next three games, Sonic would only be appearing on Nintendo hardware. The reaction from video games journalists and enthusiasts was one of quiet puzzlement. As Edge magazine wryly commented, it was hard to see which party was supposed to benefit from the deal.

In the halcyon early days of the Wii, this would have been a canny move, but Nintendo had been paying the price for under-supporting its breakout success during the second half of its life, and sales of the Wii U successor console had been abysmal as a consequence. The company had initially planned to sell 9 million units by the end of the 2013 financial year, but would eventually have to reduce this target by 70%, as performance tracked significantly below the numbers achieved by the Dreamcast over a decade earlier. Nintendo's 3DS handheld had established a foothold in that market, and the firm's mountainous cash reserves could allow it to absorb any number of home console flops, but Nintendo were far from a compelling business partner.

From a Japanese perspective, the decision was slightly more rational. Nintendo were committed to producing machines that would reach Japanese families, and Sega rightly predicted that Sony and Microsoft's forthcoming premium-price new hardware would have difficulty gaining traction in this mobile-centred market. But serving Sonic's Japanese interests was denying him the chance to build on his gradually reviving stock with the western public. A high-profile release on the imminent Playstation 4 or Xbox One machines would have drawn attention to the brand, but was now not to be.

Although Takashi Iizuka would certainly have been involved in the decision to tie Sonic to Nintendo, his Sonic Team approached the situation rationally, with a carefully calibrated approach. The first of the three exclusive titles was the next instalment of the Olympics juggernaut, but for the second, Sonic Team were obliged to deliver a core Sonic title on a system which made the Sega Saturn look like a roaring success. Money would unquestionably have changed hands in securing the deal, and the result was effectively a game which Sega were paid to make. Rather than continue the *Sonic Unleashed* style, the developers decided on a more experimental vision for this lower-profile title.

Sonic Lost World, released in October 2013, continued what had become the house style under Iizuka. Sonic and a cut-scene only Tails became entangled in Eggman's attempt to enslave a group of mysterious creatures, the Deadly Six. These under-explored villains predictably turned the tables on the scientist, converting his latest invention to empower themselves while destroying the world, and Eggman was forced to accept Sonic's help in halting their menace. While the scripting team did their best with such a thin concept, the results were wholly uninvolving, and added to the impression of a disposable effort.

Key Game

Sonic Lost World

Release : 2013

Origin : Japan

Global Sales : 0.21m

Metacritic Review Average : 63%

The gameplay itself was an odd hybrid, with Sonic making his way through a variety of cylindrical levels. On first sight of the game, fans initially defended it against allegations of borrowing from *Super Mario Galaxy*'s localised gravity spheres by pointing to strong similarities with the fish-eye lens of the scrapped *Sonic X-Treme*. They were slightly undercut by Iizuka's admission that his junior staff had not heard of the 1996 title, and were in fact under instructions to mimic the Nintendo game.

The hedgehog's controls had slowly gained in complexity over the years, but *Sonic Lost World* marked a significant step up even compared to the intricacies of *Sonic Unleashed*'s approach. Two different handling models were implemented, depending on whether a 'Run' button is held. The idea was to allow for slow-paced platforming interspersed by bursts of speed, but the results went against the grain of what was expected from Sonic, and there were severe balancing issues with the game's difficulty.

For the first time, a Sonic title had significant gameplay changes added after release through a downloadable patch, making extra lives easier to come by. The adjustment to the game disk content also allowed the returning Wisps to be deployed through conventional controls, instead of the whimsy of the Wii U joypad touchscreen.

In another first, Dimps' handheld reinterpretation of the title proved more enjoyable than the main game. The smaller firm had finally made the leap to fully-3D gameplay, and the resulting slow-paced adventure sometimes charmingly invoked memories of the 8-bit titles. The lack of effort in the home game was embodied by its lacklustre level selection, which was mainly based around the jaw-dropingly clichéd ice zone, fire zone, casino zone standards.

On the surface, *Sonic Lost World* enjoyed respectable sales considering the limited proliferation of its host platforms, but deeper analysis revealed a different picture. The bulk of copies shifted were of the lower-profile 3DS release, with the Sonic Team version of the title selling less than 100,000 copies in the key American market. Reviews were unenthusiastic, finding the game fiddly and overcomplicated. Adding to these problems, the once-unstoppable Olympic sub-brand appeared to be reaching the end of its natural life, with *Mario & Sonic at the Sochi 2014 Olympic Winter Games* barely troubling the charts

With one more game remaining in the Nintendo deal, the franchise seemed to have lapsed into a downward spiral, but 2014 brought an unexpected twist in the tale. This saw the official introduction of a separate western conception of Sonic, which would sit side-by-side with Iizuka's vision. Sega of America was spearheading the initiative, with Sonic Team's consent, under the umbrella heading of *Sonic Boom*. Building on their increased creative control and brand management experience, the western Sega groups had worked to develop a new TV show of eleven-minute CG-animated episodes, staring a redesigned Sonic, Tails, Knuckles, Amy and Eggman.

Fifty two instalments of the animation had been commissioned from French studio OuiDo, being scheduled for broadcast in several territories during the second half of the year. For the most part, the existing western voice actors were involved in the series, with one change in performer, for Tails.

The tone of the series was described as light-hearted, without any running plots from episode to episode. Radically, the series would be accompanied by an original console action title, initially earmarked for release on the Wii U and 3DS. The game was in development at US firm Big Red Button, which had been founded by veterans of Sony's Naughty Dog studio. Entertainingly, this company was now home to Christian Senn, a designer who had been employed on *Sonic X*-Treme until its cancellation.

While representatives of the developer were keen to reference previous titles such as *Sonic Adventure* in their description of how the game would play, it was difficult to relate any existing conception of the character to the approach seen in the initial teaser video.

Key Game

Sonic Boom

Release : 2014

Origin : USA

Global Sales : N/A

Metacritic Review Average : N/A

The game sported a radically different visual style, having more in common with Sony's *Crash Bandicoot* than previous Sonic games. The Naughty Dog influence was particularly strong in the character redesigns, distinguished by sports tape binding on their limbs, and displaying much more divergent silhouettes. In particular, Knuckles was bulked up to near-human proportions, in order to better communicate his status as the team's brawler.

Long-established Sonic concepts such as Chaos Emeralds had no place in the reboot, with liaison between the studios involved ensuring consistency of elements. Evolution of the *Sonic Boom* style had obviously not been frictionless. Big Red Button's CEO Bob Rafei described in an interview how Takashi Iizuka had been physically unable to look at some of the more radical proposals for Sonic's appearance, which had included giving the character fur, scales or clothes.

Sega staff being interviewed at the press launch of the *Sonic Boom* initiative were keen to make clear that it had nothing to do with Sonic Team's output, with Iizuka's organisation continuing to work on console games in its own established style. While some saw this as a fallback option in the event of *Sonic Boom* proving to be a failure, it was clear that the divergence in the global marketplace had forced a split in the approach taken to Sonic. Just as in 1991, the individual arms of Sega were free to pursue their own artistic visions for the character.

Epilogue

Looking back across the first 23 years of Sonic's life, the hedgehog appears to have come full circle, with the dawn of the next chapter in the character's story finding him in a remarkably similar position to his 1991 debut.

The Mega Drive years were marked by a headlong sprint by Sega to keep pace with the imaginations of Naoto Ôshima, Yuji Naka and Hirokazu Yusahara, with Sega of America and its Japanese counterpart struggling to match the lightning-in-a-bottle output of the original Sonic Team. In Asia, the US and Europe, rival conceptions and legends of Sonic were forged to build locally-applicable trappings around the templates that the games provided. Innumerable spin-offs and tie-ins bloomed in an uncontrolled fashion, with Sega unable to believe its luck at creating such an inherently appealing character.

The stumbles of the Saturn eroded Sonic's fortunes, but brought professionalism and control, with Sonic Team asserting its right to the final say on the direction of its creation. The result was *Sonic Adventure*, the last title from the character's creators, which revitalised him and gave him a clear place in a vastly-changed console landscape. Under Naka's control, the sixth generation of consoles saw a clear drive to embed Sonic in a quasi-real-world setting, best encapsulated by the *Sonic X* cartoon, as the hedgehog was briefly released from the development budget constraints caused by Sega's near-bankruptcy.

With the departure of Naka, Sonic stumbled, with his brand finally tarnished by the limited resources available to create his adventures. The thunderbolt creative success of *Sonic Unleashed* gave him an expected burst of energy, and producer Takashi Iizuka was able to build a smaller-scale, but more solid, conception of the character. Sonic was a lesser hero, enjoying simpler quests, but the injuries he'd sustained from Sega's financial troubles were healing.

This brings us to the present day. The realities of the global marketplace call for two radically different visions of Sonic, with Sonic Team's crusading animal-protector appealing to Japanese children, while the travelling adventurer being sketched into life by OuiDo and Big Red Button is better-placed to reach their western counterparts.

What's most striking is the sheer momentum of the character. Sonic The Hedgehog was created to launch Sega into the international console market. And now, with Sega hardware a memory, the company itself having narrowly escaped bankruptcy, and the global video game marketplace changed beyond all recognition, he's still running and gearing up for his next adventure.

Unstoppable.

Author's Thanks

The origins of this book lie in a series of articles written for the online portal *Noise To Signal*. The website served up an eclectic mix of criticism and enthusiasm on a variety of niche topics. Users were normally drawn by one particular update that chimed with their own interests, and would end up staying after being drawn into fields that they knew nothing about. A series of essays on a cartoon video game character was fairly typical of the site's content, but *Sonic Adventures* was usually comprehensive, looking at trends in the gradual evolution of the character, instead of a one-off historical examination. Five years later, the hedgehog has a few more sprints and stumbles under his belt, and the subject seemed ripe for another look.

I'm extremely grateful to the Noise To Signal editorial team; Jonathan Capps, John Hoare, Tanya Jones, Michael Lacey, Seb Patrick, Phil Reed, Austin Ross and Ian Symes, for their invaluable help in writing those original articles. All errors that remain are entirely my own. Thanks also to those who offered their encouragement during the rewriting process; Joey Cannon, Andrea Clement, Scott Lyons and Danny Stephenson.

The beautiful cover which graces the physical release is by YF Studio; you can find more information on their work at yakageforce.co.uk. The text is set in Geo Sans Light, a public-domain font created by Manfred Klein, with layout by Seb Patrick.

This book is respectfully dedicated to the memory of Ray The Flying Squirrel.

Julian Hazeldine

April 2014

Index

The following list documents the media in this book by year, noting the medium and creators involved. Minor cameos, edutainment software and some mobile titles have been omitted for clarity. For games, launch window formats only shown.

Where one game has been released for multiple formats, one listing is presented. Where titles with the same name offer significantly different experiences, these are shown as multiple entries.

Sonic The Hedgehog (1993-Present)	Comic, USA	Archie	p34
Sonic The Comic (1993-2002)	Comic, UK	Fleetway	p35
Sonic The Hedgehog in Robotnik's Laboratory *et al* (Four Novels)	Book, UK	"Martin Adams" & Virgin Publishing	p24
Metal City Mayhem *et al* (Six Choose-Your-Own Adventure Books)	Book, UK	Puffin	p25
Sonic The Hedgehog CD	Game, Mega CD	Sega Enterprises	p16
The Adventures of Sonic The Hedgehog (66 Episodes)	TV, USA	DIC Entertainment	p27
Sonic The Hedgehog Chaos	Game, Master System/Game Gear	Aspect	p31
Sonic Spinball	Game, Mega Drive	STI	p35
Sonic The Hedgehog (AKA *SatAM*) (26 Episodes)	TV, USA	DIC Entertainment	p33

1994

Sonic The Hedgehog 3	Game, Mega Drive	Sonic Team & STI	p28
Sonic Drift	Game, Game Gear	Sega Enterprises	p31
Sonic The Poster Magazine (Nine issues)	Comic, UK	Fleetway	p36
Sonic Special (Quarterly, 1994-1996)	Comic, USA	Archie	p34
Sonic & Knuckles	Game, Mega Drive	Sonic Team & STI	p38
Sonic The Hedgehog: Triple Trouble	Game, Game Gear	Aspect	p31

1995

Sonic Drift 2	Game, Game Gear	Sega Enterprises	p31
Tails' Skypatrol	Game, Game Gear	SIMS & JSH	p31
Knuckles Chaotix	Game, 32X	Sega AM7	p47
Tails' Adventure	Game, Game Gear	Aspect	p31
Sonic Labyrinth	Game, Game Gear	Minato Giken	p31

1996

Sonic The Fighters (AKA Sonic Championship)	Game, Arcade	Sega AM2	p53

Sonic The Hedgehog (2 Episodes)	TV, Japan	Studio Pierrot	p54
Sonic Blast	Game, Game Gear	Aspect	p31
Sonic 3D Blast	Game, Mega Drive/Saturn (1997)	Traveller's Tales	p45

1997

Knuckles The Echidna (1997-2000)	Comic, USA	Archie	p34
Sonic Super Specials (Quarterly 1997-2001)	Comic, USA	Archie	p34
Sonic Jam	Game, Saturn	Sonic Team	p57
Sonic R	Game, Saturn	Traveller's Tales	p58

1998

Sonic Adventure	Game, Dreamcast	Sonic Team	p61

1999

Sonic Underground (40 Episodes)	TV, USA/France	DIC Entertainment	p66
Sonic The Hedgehog Pocket Adventure	Game, Neo Geo Pocket Colour	Dimps	p67

2000

Sonic Shuffle	Game, Dreamcast	Hudson Soft	p67

2001

Sonic Adventure 2	Game, Dreamcast/Gamecube	Sonic Team USA	p68
Sonic Advance	Game, Game Boy Advance	Dimps	p73

2002

Sonic Advance 2	Game, Game Boy Advance	Dimps	p74

2003

Sonic Pinball Party	Game, Game Boy Advance	Sonic Team	p75
Sonic Heroes	Game, PS2/Gamecube/Xbox	Sonic Team USA	p78
Sonic X Series 1 (26 Episodes)	TV, Japan/France	TMS Entertainment	p75

2004

Sonic X Series 2 (26 Episodes)	TV, Japan/France	TMS Entertainment	p76
Sonic Battle	Game, Game Boy Advance	Sonic Team	p75
Sonic Advance 3	Game, Game Boy Advance	Dimps	p74

2005

Sonic X Series 3 (26 Episodes)	TV, Japan/France	TMS Entertainment	p77

Sonic Rush	Game, Nintendo DS	Dimps	p83
Shadow The Hedgehog	Game, PS2/Gamecube/Xbox	Sonic Team USA	p81
Sonic X (2005-2008)	Comic, USA	Archie	p34

2006

Sonic Riders	Game, PS2/Gamecube/Xbox	Sonic Team	p84
Sonic The Hedgehog *AKA Sonic The Hedgehog [2006]*	Game, Xbox 360/PS3	Sonic Team	p85
Sonic Rivals	Game, PSP	Backbone Entertainment	p93

2007

Sonic and the Secret Rings	Game, Wii	Sonic Team	p92
Sonic Rush Adventure	Game, Nintendo DS	Dimps	p93
Mario & Sonic at the Olympic Games	Game, Wii/Nintendo DS	Sega Sports R&D	p94
Sonic Rivals 2	Game, PSP	Backbone Entertainment	p94

2008

Sega Superstars Tennis	Game, Xbox 360/PS3	Sumo Digital	p95

Sonic Riders: Zero Gravity	Game, Gamecube	Sonic Team	p85
Sonic Chronicles: The Dark Brotherhood	Game, Nintendo DS	Bioware	p95
Sonic Unleashed (AKA Sonic World Adventure)	Game, Xbox 360/PS3/Wii/PS2	Sonic Team & Dimps (Wii & PS2)	p97

2009

Sonic Universe (2009-Present)	Comic, USA	Archie	p34
Sonic and the Black Knight	Game, Wii	Sonic Team	p102
Mario & Sonic at the Olympic Winter Games	Game, Wii/Nintendo DS	Sega Sports R&D	p95

2010

Sonic & Sega All-Stars Racing	Game, Xbox 360/PS3/Wii/DS	Sumo Digital	p103
Sonic The Hedgehog 4 Episode 1	Game, Xbox 360/PS3/Wii/iOS	Dimps	p105
Sonic Free Riders	Game, Xbox Kinnect	Sonic Team	p103
Sonic Colours	Game, Wii/Nintendo DS	Sonic Team & Dimps (DS)	p108

2011

Mario & Sonic at the London 2012 Olympic Games	Game, Wii/Nintendo DS	Sega Sports Japan	p95
Sonic Generations	Game, Xbox 360/PS3	Sonic Team	p112
Sonic Generations	Game, Nintendo 3DS	Dimps	p113

2012

Sonic The Hedgehog 4 Episode 2	Game, Xbox 360/PS3/iOS	Dimps	p115
Sonic Jump	Game, iOS/Android	Hardlight	p120
Sonic & All-Stars Racing Transformed	Game, 360/PS3/Wii U/PS Vita/3DS	Sumo Digital	p120

2013

Sonic Dash	Game, iOS/Android	Hardlight	p120
Sonic: Lost World	Game, Wii U/3DS	Sonic Team & Dimps (3DS)	p122
Mario & Sonic at the Sochi 2014 Olympic Winter Games	Game, Wii U /3DS	Sega Sports Japan	p95

2014

Sonic Boom	Game, Wii U/3DS	Big Red Button & Sanzaru games (3DS)	p124
Sonic Boom (52	TV, USA/France	OuiDo!	p123

Episodes)

www.ingramcontent.com/pod-product-compliance
Lightning Source LLC
Chambersburg PA
CBHW071212050326
40689CB00011B/2310